MOLLY NESS &
KATIE PACE MILES

THE SCIENCE OF READING IN PRACTICE

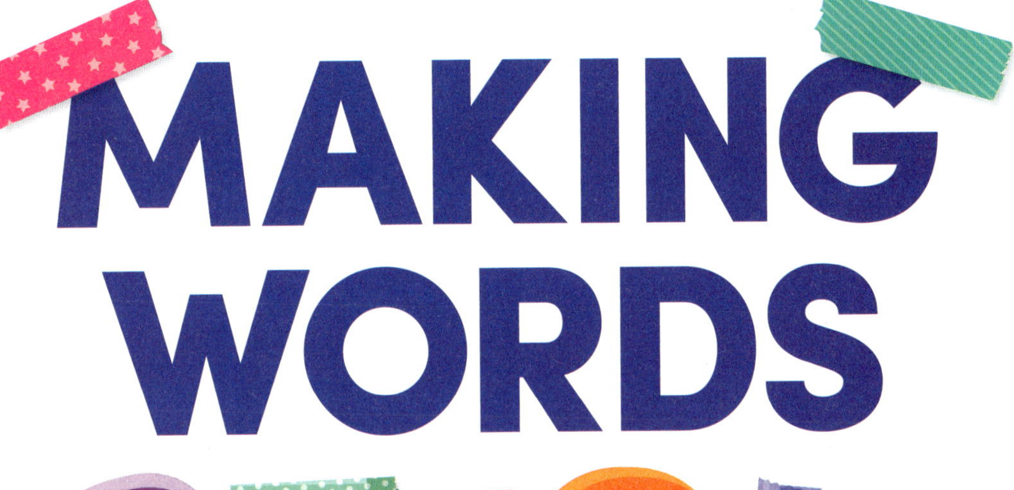

MAKING WORDS STICK

A Four-Step Instructional Routine to Power Up Orthographic Mapping

SCHOLASTIC

Dedication

To our families, who tolerate us, cheer us on, and forgive us when our professional passion detracts from our parenting and partnering times. In particular, to our children—Callie, Georgie, and Henry—who challenge and inspire us daily.

Senior Vice President and Publisher: Tara Welty
Editorial Director: Sarah Longhi
Editor-in-Chief: Raymond Coutu
Production Editor: Danny Miller
Assistant Editor: Samantha Unger
Cover Design: Tannaz Fassihi
Interior Design: Maria Lilja

Photos throughout © courtesy of Molly Ness and Katie Pace Miles. Additional photos and cover art © Getty Images and Shutterstock.com.

Credits: 31: Word chart "CPB Sight Words (The First 100 Words)" by Clarence Green, Kathleen Keogh, and Julia Prout from "The CPB Sight Words: A New Research-Based High-Frequency Wordlist for Early Reading Instruction" published in *The Reading Teacher*, Volume 78, no. 1. Copyright © International Reading Association. Reprinted by permission of John Wiley & Sons, Inc.; 32: covers and pages from *Laugh-A-Lot Phonics Short Vowels: Jen Pen; Clue Club Decodable Mysteries Book 3: The Case of Bigfoot on the Run*; and *Nonfiction Phonics Readers: SET 2: Long Vowels, Digraphs & More: A Whale Can Wave* © 2023 & 2024 by Lefty's Editorial Services. Used by permission of Scholastic Inc.; 45: cover and pages from *Nonfiction Phonics Readers: SET 2: Long Vowels, Digraphs & More: This Moth* © 2023 by Lefty's Editorial Services. Used by permission of Scholastic Inc.; 48: *Scholastic Ready4Reading®* "Scope & Sequence" © 2023 by Scholastic Inc. All rights reserved.

Printed in the U.S.A.

ISBN 978-1-5461-7645-9

3 4 5 6 7 8 9 10 40 34 33 32 31 30 29 28 27 26

Scholastic Inc., 557 Broadway, New York, NY 10012

CONTENTS

Foreword by Jan Hasbrouck 7

Introduction 9

Our Stories 10

Why We Wrote This Book 12

CHAPTER 1: **How the Brain Maps Words** 15

What the Heck Is Orthographic Mapping? 16

What Happens in the Brain When We Map Words? 19

In What Ways Do We Typically Read Words? 22

How Do Children Grow as Word Readers and Spellers? 24

CHAPTER 2: **The Lowdown on High-Frequency Words** 29

Understanding the Many Categories of Words 29

Making High-Frequency Words Stick 34

CHAPTER 3: **An Instructional Routine for Making Words Stick** 39

An Overview of Our Routine 39

The Menu of Activities for Grades K–5 46

CHAPTER 4: **Making Words Stick in Grades K and 1** 51
Pre-Alphabetic Readers 51
Partial-Alphabetic Readers 52
The Tension Between Reading and Spelling in Grades K and 1 54
The Instructional Routine for Grades K and 1 55
A Menu of Activities 55
Place Your Order 56
Activity Instructions and Scripts 57
Step 1: See & Say 58
Step 2: Segment & Spell 63
Step 3: Study & Suss Out 69
Step 4: Search & Stick 81

CHAPTER 5: **Making Words Stick in Grades 2 and 3** 85
Full-Alphabetic Readers 85
The Tension Between Reading and Spelling in Grades 2 and 3 86
The Instructional Routine for Grades 2 and 3 88
A Menu of Activities 88
Place Your Order 89
Activity Instructions and Scripts 90
Step 1: See & Say 91
Step 2: Segment & Spell 95
Step 3: Study & Suss Out 99
Step 4: Search & Stick 112

CHAPTER 6: **Making Words Stick in Grades 4 and 5** ... 117

Consolidated Alphabetic Readers ... 117

The Tension Between Reading and Spelling in Grades 4 and 5 ... 119

The Instructional Routine for Grades 4 and 5 ... 120

A Menu of Activities ... 120

Place Your Order ... 121

Activity Instructions and Scripts ... 122

Step 1: See & Say ... 123

Step 2: Segment & Spell ... 125

Step 3: Study & Suss Out ... 128

Step 4: Search & Stick ... 136

Conclusion ... 140

Appendix ... 142

References ... 154

Index ... 157

ACKNOWLEDGMENTS

Thank you to the entire Scholastic team, who shaped this book and launched it into the world, especially Sarah Longhi and Tara Welty. We are particularly appreciative of the wisdom, humor, and guidance of Ray Coutu. Thank you to our invaluable friend and colleague Dr. Carolyn Strom for her feedback. We are deeply grateful to Dr. Jan Hasbrouck for the time she spent reviewing and generously endorsing this book. We are collectively better teachers, researchers, and literacy advocates because of Andrew Fletcher, Doug Distefano, Justin Browning, Jacqueline Shannon, and our Reading League friends and network. A special thanks to Chistina Oliver, Emily Van Houten, Mady Glickman, and Yascara Maldonado at The Reading Institute and to the staff and students in the Advanced Certificate in Reading Science program at Brooklyn College, CUNY. Finally, we are indebted to Dr. Linnea Ehri for her scholarship, mentorship, and leadership in the field of reading science.

FOREWORD by Jan Hasbrouck

I decided early on in my life that I wanted to be a teacher. Ultimately, my dream came true, although in a different way than I had planned. I thought I would be a classroom teacher, but instead I've focused my entire career on the teaching of reading. I worked as a reading specialist and then as an instructional coach before becoming a professor and researcher. These days, I am lucky to still be working in education, consulting with educators around the world who support literacy. I look back on my long career and feel such gratitude that I made this choice. Helping students learn to read—and supporting teachers doing this challenging work—continues to bring me joy.

Even after 50 years in the field, I find myself eager to learn about the best evidence-based practices that help every student become a reader (and writer). Everyone devoted to students' literacy development must continue learning because teaching students to read and write is complex, and for many of those students it is a serious challenge. And there continues to be a lot to learn! Researchers are always discovering ways the brain learns to read and the best instructional practices to support that learning.

One of the many amazing aspects of skillful reading is the brain's ability to effortlessly recognize words in print. In *Making Words Stick*, Dr. Molly Ness and Dr. Katie Pace Miles state that the average reader has cognitively stored approximately 30,000 to 70,000 words, available for instantaneous, precognitive identification. The style of the letters can change, the size of them can change, and it makes no difference! We see a printed word that we have learned, and we immediately know what it says and what it means (although we may need context to confirm the meaning). That one single aspect of reading is simply mind-boggling! How in the world is it even possible?

Dr. Linnea Ehri is credited with originating the theory about how words are stored for retrieval in long-term memory, which she has called "orthographic mapping." She and others have conducted decades of research into that process, and they have identified optimal, strategic ways to help students map words into their brains for instant, accurate recognition.

Helping students acquire a mental lexicon of instantly recognized "sight words" is necessary for fluent, skillful reading and for successful spelling. Sadly, though, many teachers were taught to encourage students to "memorize" words, using methods that more recent evidence has shown to be much less effective. We want all students to know a lot of sight words. If memorization is not the right way, what should we do instead?

We are all in luck! Molly Ness and Katie Pace Miles have written a book filled with specific, easy-to-follow, classroom-friendly instructional routines and fun, motivational activities for K–5 students to acquire those all-important "sight words" necessary for skillful word reading, comprehension, and spelling. Molly and Katie have great respect for teachers and the highly challenging work of teaching. They are both teachers at heart. They have "walked the talk" in their own classrooms and learned a lot along the way. As evidence, early in the book, they share some ineffective methods they used early in their careers with their own students to teach them to recognize high-frequency words and to spell.

To teach skillfully, it helps to understand what is actually going on in our students' brains, but that can get overwhelmingly complicated quickly! Molly and Katie masterfully describe how the brain works to develop reading proficiency, in a clear and understandable way. They explain Dr. Ehri's theory of orthographic mapping and connect it to instruction that supports learning (and explain why rote memorization of words is NOT the way to go!).

I'll bet most teachers' favorite part of this wonderful book will be the many engaging, age-appropriate, and effective routines and activities to help all learners succeed.

You have a treasure in your hand! This book will enable so many students to learn words with ease and use those words to read and write skillfully and confidently. I am grateful to Molly and Katie for it and confident you will feel the same.

—**JAN HASBROUCK, Ph.D.**, author/coeditor of *Climbing the Ladder of Reading & Writing*, *Conquering Dyslexia*, and *Student-Focused Coaching*

INTRODUCTION

Think about the words you've read today—in emails, texts, recipes, directions, newspapers, street signs, menus, social media posts, and (hopefully) a book or magazine for pleasure. What you read depends on your life circumstances and schedule. For example, if you are pursuing additional certification, coursework, or professional learning, you may be reading research studies containing statistical terms and complex vocabulary. If it's tax season, you might be wading through financial documents. And although your purposes for reading may vary, one thing remains consistent: Of all the words you encounter on a daily basis, you rarely decode any of them. You instantaneously recognize the vast majority of them.

Now, there are certainly a few exceptions: proper nouns, unfamiliar technical terms, and obscure, infrequently used terms. (For Molly, it's words on her Page-a-Day calendar, such as *pogonip*, which means "a dense winter fog." For Katie, it's the Word of the Day listserv she's on, where she'll be greeted with terms such as *sehnsucht*, which means "yearning or wistful longing.")

The average reader instantly and effortlessly recognizes 30,000 to 70,000 words, with no need to decode them or sound them out (Mather & Jaffe, 2021). But that does not mean that decoding wasn't necessary for that to happen—or more specifically, to get those words into memory. In fact, it begets the question: How did all of those words become instantly recognizable? The answer lies in the process of orthographic mapping (Ehri, 2000, 2005, 2014, 2022, 2023).

Making Words Stick will help you understand orthographic mapping as a cognitive process that readers use to store and retrieve words. We explain how proficient readers integrate a word's pronunciation, spelling, and meaning so they can instantly recognize it, leading to fluent, effortless reading and deep comprehension. (See Chapter 1 for a complete explanation of orthographic mapping.) Not only will we convince you of the necessity of orthographic mapping for reading success, but we will also give you an instructional routine that you can use with any reading program or phonics scope and sequence. (See Chapter 3 for an overview of the routine and Chapters 4 through 6 for ways to apply it across grade levels.) Our goal is to provide you with the perfect balance of information you need and the tools you can use tomorrow.

Our Stories

But before we get into the nitty-gritty of theory and practice, we invite you to take a stroll down memory lane as we revisit our early years of teaching and events that compelled us to write this book.

Molly Is Put to the Test Teaching Spelling

In 1999, I was a first-year teacher in Oakland, California.

One quick glance at my sixth graders' writing revealed a dire need for spelling instruction. And so I began teaching it, which went something like this: I searched students' independent writing for the most frequently misspelled words. Then I'd list 10 words on the board for the whole class to see.

Molly and one of her first students

	In Class, I'd Have Students:	At Home, I'd Have Them:
Monday	Copy words from the board into their spelling notebooks.	Write each word three times correctly in their spelling notebooks.
Tuesday	Discuss the meaning of each word.	Put the words into alphabetical order.
Wednesday	Select five words and write five sentences containing them.	Complete two worksheets: a spelling-list crossword puzzle and a spelling word hunt.
Thursday	Play review games to prepare for Friday's spelling test.	Study for the test.
Friday	Take the spelling test.	Share results (hopefully!) with parents/caregivers.

Initially, I was pleased with my instruction. I had lots of positive data to record in my grade book, columns of 9/10 and 10/10. My students appeared to be hard at work, as they diligently copied their words, used them in sentences, and regurgitated them on worksheets. My spelling routine ran like a well-oiled machine.

But over time, the cracks appeared. For example, the student who had perfect 10s in my grade book couldn't spell *because* or *girl* the next week in independent writing. Rebecca Putnam (2017) called the phenomenon of correct spelling for tests but failure to generalize that knowledge to other writing "Friday test, Monday miss." I realized that my students weren't transferring spellings largely because I was not following a clear progression of linguistic concepts or spelling rules. Instead, I was randomly picking disconnected words and putting them on the weekly spelling lists. Even worse, when I got the dreaded question, "Ms. Ness, how do you spell (insert word)?," my response was "Look it up in the dictionary." I was stunted by my lack of understanding of English language structures because I was not providing the phonetic or morphological support that my students needed.

Katie's Low Point With High-Frequency Words

A few years later and a thousand miles east, I was a bright-eyed, idealistic kindergarten teacher.

Katie's first "school picture"

Armed with my chalk (this was before Smartboards!), clipboard, lanyard with a stopwatch, and laminated ID badge, I co-taught 18 six-year-olds in Denver, Colorado. My heart was full watching their exponential growth, and I belly laughed daily at their priceless comments. I nodded along as my co-teacher confidently taught the Dolch List of high-frequency words (1936). I followed her system: Write the first set of words on index cards, punch a hole in the corner of each card, and fasten the cards with a ring binder. Show each card to students individually and have them read the word aloud. Retire words that they automatically recognize after three correct readings (usually over three days). Keep missed words on the ring of cards. Keep retired words in a recipe-card box to remind students of words they have mastered. Replace the retired words with new unfamiliar words, and repeat the process the next day.

Each day, I gathered students in small groups at our reading table, allotting precious instructional time to drilling those high-frequency words. Some cards moved off of binder rings and into their individual recipe-card boxes, while other cards grew dingy and crumpled as they traveled back and forth from home to school. Boxes were proudly displayed—like trophies—at curriculum night and parent-teacher conferences.

As a rookie teacher, I was perplexed as to why some students' boxes were bursting at the seams by the end of the year, while others were practically empty. Little did I know that a decade later, this instructional approach would inspire a body of my research!

Why We Wrote This Book

Of course, hindsight is 20/20, and we can now look back and pinpoint the gaps in our knowledge and the errors in our ineffective, albeit well-intended, instruction. Katie didn't systematically teach students to analyze parts of the word. If Molly's students hadn't mastered how to read or spell high-frequency words, she reminded them, "Practice your words at home tonight" or asked them, "Did you study for your spelling test?" Rarely did we explain advanced phonetic concepts—such as when to use *-ge* vs. *-dge* and the schwa sound—or spelling rules, such as, "Words in English don't end in *v* so you add an *e*." Instead, we relied on rote memorization and the hope that after our students saw, heard, and copied words, they'd automatically store them in memory and access them later for reading and writing.

Today, we try to grant ourselves grace and be mindful of the "know better, do better" philosophy. We didn't have explicit professional training on phoneme-grapheme correspondences early in our careers. We didn't understand the nuances between common terms such as "high-frequency words" and "sight words," and "phonemic awareness" and "phonics." And we were certainly unaware of the reading brain's developing neurological circuits.

Those lingering questions about what didn't work in our classrooms led us to study reading development as doctoral students. And while pursuing our advanced degrees, we learned about the research confirming our instincts as classroom teachers. Remember Katie's observation that some students' word boxes were empty, while others were full? Researcher David Share (1999, 2011) noted that it may take 1 to 4 exposures for new words to be cemented in a reader's memory, but neurodivergent students may need many more exposures. This book provides numerous activities to support students in need of additional word-analysis practice.

As former classroom teachers and current academics and teacher educators, we are committed to translating research into practice. Though orthographic mapping has a substantial and rigorous research base, until recently, few practitioners knew about it. We aim to move it out of academic journals and into the hands of those who need it and deserve it most: classroom teachers, literacy coaches, and school leaders. In this book, we explain this cognitive process by which we learn to read, and we offer practical ideas for immediate classroom application.

Final Thoughts

We know you'll learn a lot about reading development and reading instruction from this book, including the following:

- First, you'll learn about the interplay between and among brain regions and how neural networks develop reading proficiency.
- Second, you'll become familiar with how orthographic mapping occurs and the research behind it.
- Third, you'll be ready to apply our four-step instructional routine described in detail in Chapter 3, and its related activities, to support students in word identification. Here's a preview!

Step	Goal
① See & Say	Students see the word and then make a phonological representation of the word, in order to access the word's sound structure. Simply put, they hear the word and say the word aloud while looking at it.
② Segment & Spell	Students identify the word's grapheme-phoneme correspondences by mapping the word's sounds to its letters.
③ Study & Suss Out	Students explore the meaning of the word and its usage. They understand multiple meanings of the words, as well as its syntax and semantics.
④ Search & Stick	Students move toward automatically recognizing the word, as well as instantly retrieving the word when it appears in text.

- And fourth, you'll recognize that students' knowledge of a word's phonology, orthography, and meaning is the key to helping them map words in the mind.

As you read, you'll see that each chapter ends with specific takeaways. Look throughout the book for "Did You Know?" sidebars containing compelling facts about our brains, our language, and literacy development. Let's make words stick!

Terms to Remember	
Decoding	The ability to translate a word from print to speech, usually by employing knowledge of letter-sound relationships. Also, the act of deciphering a new word by sounding it out.
Morphology/ Morphological	The study of the internal structure of words and of word formation; how meaningful parts of a word come together to create a word's meaning.
Neural Networks	Groups of neurons in the brain that send signals to one another to process information.
Neurodivergent	Relating to the many different ways our brains function. This removes the stigma associated with learning differences that are often tagged as learning disabilities.
Orthographic Mapping (OM)	A cognitive process that facilitates the storage of words in long-term memory by connecting a specific word's spelling to its pronunciation and meaning.
Orthography	The study of how words are written, and the particular rules that dictate their structure and spelling. It is a key component of reading, decoding, and spelling.
Phonemic Awareness	The ability to identify and manipulate sounds in spoken words.
Phonetic	Relating to speech sounds. When young students spell phonetically, they "sound out" the word they want to write and record a reasonable letter/letter combination for each sound they hear. They might write: "APL" for apple or "BIC" for bike.
Phonics	The relationship between letters and the sounds they represent, and how to teach children to use that knowledge to read, write, and spell by matching the sounds of spoken language with the letters/letter combinations that represent those sounds.
Phonological Awareness	The ability to recognize and manipulate the sound structure of language, including syllables, onsets and rimes, rhyming, alliteration, and phonemic awareness.
Scope & Sequence	A plan detailing the skills and concepts that will be taught in a curriculum, and the order in which they will be taught.

CHAPTER 1

How the Brain Maps Words

This past summer, Molly encountered a new word while reading Nina Simon's *Mother-Daughter Murder Night* (2023). The sentence reads as follows: "She looked down at the freshly piled sand beside her, then out to the fog blanketing the slough."

Slough? Huh?

Being the research nerd that she is, Molly looked up *slough* and found it has three meanings:

Slough: As a noun, *slough* means 1) a swamp or 2) a situation characterized by a lack of progress. As a verb, it means "to shed or remove."

But knowing the definition wasn't enough. If Molly was to use the word, she needed to know its pronunciation. Was it *slough* like *cough*? Or *slough* like *dough*? Or even *slough* like *rough*? In fact, there are multiple ways to pronounce the *-ough* pattern, as shown below!

The letters "ough" can be pronounced at least six ways in English. How did this happen?

cough	→	*off*	though	→	*oh*
rough	→	*uff*	bought	→	*aw*
through	→	*ew*	drought	→	*ow*

At her favorite dictionary website, Dictionary.com, she clicked an icon to hear it pronounced. Turns out, there are regional differences in *slough*'s pronunciation: New Yorkers would likely rhyme it with *cow*, but Canadians and West Coasters pronounce it more as *slew*. Now that she made connections between the word's spelling, pronunciation, and meaning, Molly automatically recognized *slough* every time she encountered it in the remainder of the book; she had gone through the cognitive process of orthographic mapping to store *slough* in her mental Rolodex of words.

What the Heck Is Orthographic Mapping?

Molly's experience is a good example of how we store words in memory through orthographic mapping (OM). OM is the process by which the letters in the spelling of a word are bound to the sounds those letters make. That spelling-to-pronunciation connection is the "glue."

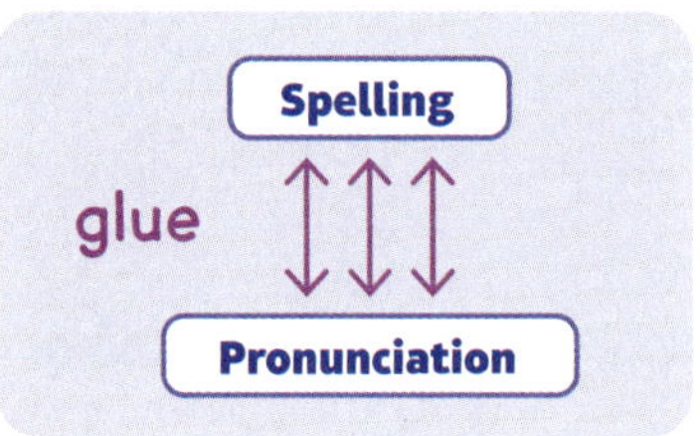

When we link the meaning of the word to its spelling and pronunciation, we're on our way to storing the word in long-term memory (Ehri, 1992, 1998, 2000, 2005, 2014, 2022, 2023).

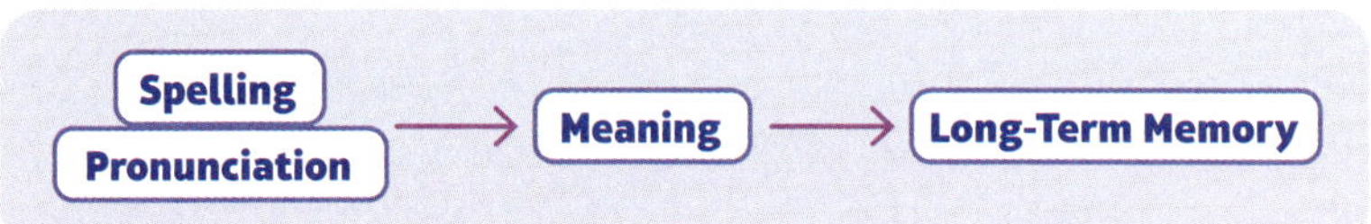

It's important to note that all students need word-analysis skills, not just beginning readers. Molly is certainly a proficient reader, and yet she had to clarify the pronunciation and meaning of *slough* to store it in her memory. Also, orthographic mapping applies to words of all kinds, not just high-frequency words (Ehri, 2022). *Slough* is certainly not a high-frequency word!

Watch Molly and Katie explain orthographic mapping and why it's important.

Orthographic Mapping and Word Reading

Reading researcher Dr. Linnea Ehri first wrote about orthographic mapping two decades ago (1992, 1998). She developed this theory based on the findings from her many studies involving readers at various points in their development. She explained that words are stored in long-term memory through a cognitive process of mapping the spelling of a word to its pronunciation and meaning (Ehri, 1992, 1998, 2000, 2005, 2014, 2020, 2022, 2023). In other words, readers break a word into its letter units, segment the sounds of those units, and blend the letter-sound units to pronounce the word. That segmenting and blending process is the glue that sticks the word in memory, and the meaning more securely anchors it there. The more a reader encounters and decodes the word, the more securely it becomes stored, and the easier it is to retrieve.

Did You Know?
While there are 44 phonemes in the English language, there are over 250 ways to spell them (Honig et al., 2018)!

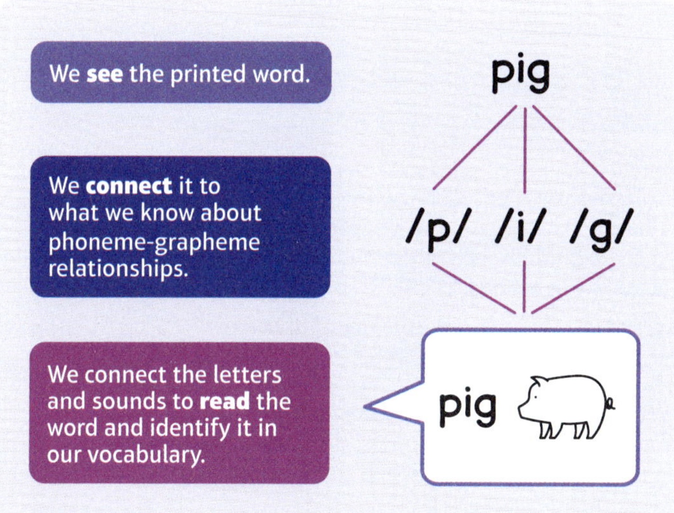

Throughout the book, we use / / to denote a particular sound. For example, for the word *cool*, /c/ indicates the first sound made by the *c*, and /ool/ indicates the sound made by the remaining letters.

The Tension Between Reading and Spelling

But orthographic mapping isn't just for recognizing or decoding words; it is also for spelling, or encoding, them. Ehri (2020) describes the relationship between reading and spelling as two sides of the same coin. Timothy Shanahan (2022) writes that reading and spelling draw on the same well of linguistic knowledge. Katie has suggested that reading and spelling can be thought of as two opposing parts of a rubber band.

This metaphor reminds us that reading and spelling don't always develop at the same rate. Sometimes students' word reading is stronger or progresses faster than their spelling, so the rubber band is stretched further in one direction. At other points, the rubber band has equal tension to represent the synchrony of reading and spelling. Students must be able to transfer the phonetic knowledge they use for reading words to spelling. Often, students need explicit instruction and practice spelling words to store in memory the correct orthographic representation of those words. In subsequent chapters, we pick up this analogy and explain it in relation to students' literacy development.

Which Is Harder? Reading a Word or Spelling It?

Reading words is easier than spelling words! To read a word, you simply need to recognize it or recognize the letter-sounds relationships and blend them together to decode the word. When you spell, you determine which of the numerous letter combinations represent the sound you aim to spell.

For example, to reproduce the accurate spelling of the word *brain*, you need to have memorized the correct long-*a* spelling pattern, out of multiple options (i.e., *a*, *a-e*, *ai*, ay, *ei*, *eigh*, or *ey*), used in that specific word. Mather and Jaffe (2021) explain that spelling is more difficult because of orthographic memory: "Accurate spelling requires retrieval of each letter or letter combination in the correct sequence."

Orthographic Mapping and Reading Comprehension

While it may seem that OM is all about word recognition, it is a key ingredient in building reading comprehension. As students store more words in long-term memory, they increase the number of words they can read automatically by sight. Automatic word recognition enables fluent reading; students can devote mental energy to understanding—or comprehending—what they read, rather than decoding words (Miles & Ehri, 2019). The reverse is also true: When students struggle to decode words, they lose cognitive energy to comprehend continuous text.

What Happens in the Brain When We Map Words?

Molly activated multiple regions of her brain to orthographically map *slough*. Let us indulge you in a brief overview of what that looks like—or the cognitive processes that underlie reading development. In this section, we offer a clear, concise discussion of, what Gentry and Ouellette call, "the wondrous and utterly complex [human brain] containing about 85 to 120 billion cells" (2025). Equally awesome, those billions of cells have more than 160 trillion connections between them (Lilienfeld et al., 2018).

Did You Know?
The brain is ever-evolving through a process called *neuroplasticity*, meaning the brain's ability to form and organize new connections.

Let's first clarify a term often used in conversations about literacy: the reading brain. The reading brain is not so much an organ as it is a series of neural pathways that we activate and integrate to connect multiple regions of the brain. We also use the term "reading circuit" interchangeably with the reading brain (Gentry & Ouellette, 2025).

To read efficiently, our brain connects what we say (i.e., words) and what we see (i.e., text) to what words mean (Dehaene, 2009; Wolf, 2008). Our understanding of the reading circuit has evolved, thanks to functional Magnetic Resonance Imaging (fMRI). fMRI allows researchers to see neural activity of study participants via changes in blood flow to certain areas of the brain while they carry out reading-related tasks. An extensive body of research shows that proficient adult readers and typically developing emergent readers activate and coordinate neural pathways across the same brain regions (Wolf, 2008). In early reading, children's working memory is significantly taxed by their efforts

Watch Molly explain the reading brain and how it works.

to decode. As the reading process becomes more automatic and effortless, readers have more cognitive space to focus on meaning and thinking.

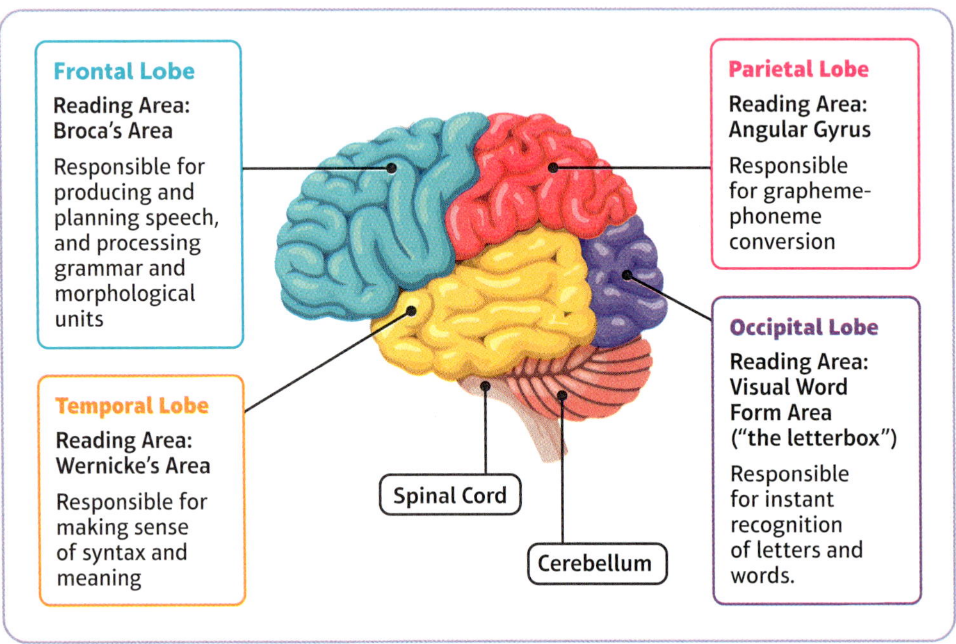

Did You Know?
Eye-tracking software indicates that proficient readers recognize sight words in about 250 milliseconds (Just & Carpenter, 1987). This is less than ¼ of a second!

The Occipital Lobe

Let's return to the word *slough* to explain how reading circuity is activated. When you encounter a written word, the first step involves visual processing. Areas of the brain's occipital lobe detect and process the shapes and visual features of letters. The Visual Word Form Area—what cognitive neuroscientist Stanislas Dehaene (2013) calls "the letterbox"—recognizes the forms of each letter in *slough*. Yet, those squiggles are a bit useless until they are converted into their associated sounds and linked to meaning.

The Parietal Lobe

To attach sounds to letter strings, the parietal lobe converts those symbols into their associated sounds. The six letters in *slough* become three phonemes: /s/ /l/ /ō/, and those phonemes are pushed together or blended to become the word *slough*. In two brain regions spanning the frontal and temporal lobes, the pronunciation of the word is consolidated and sent out for speech production.

The Temporal and Frontal Lobes

Now, we need to connect the word's visual representation and sound structure to its meaning; this occurs back in the brain's temporal lobe, specifically in Wernicke's Area, and in the frontal lobe, specifically Broca's Area. Wernicke's Area is responsible for linguistic comprehension, or the understanding of word meaning, and Broca's processes the grammatical use or syntactical use of the word. So once we understand a *slough* to be a swampy area of water, we associate it with mud, inlets, or marshes. Those associated characteristics are called "semantic relations."

In the last two decades, fMRI has allowed neuroscientists to literally see how the human brain of an expert reader functions. This work has largely confirmed beyond any doubt that expert readers are indeed able to identify sequences of letters and map them to spoken language in a fraction of a second via new neural pathways. Neuroscience has identified, with remarkable specificity, how the human brain develops and engages those capacities, not only with English, but also with dozens of other languages.

Developing the Reading Circuitry

The next time someone asks you what you do for a living, instead of saying, "I teach," say, "I change human brains," for that's exactly what happens through explicit reading instruction! Reading is the process of instantly converting otherwise meaningless symbols (i.e., letters) into something we can understand: spoken language. When we read, we build neural pathways through a process of neuroplasticity, the brain's ability to change its structure and function because of stimuli. Dehaene (2013) says, "Compared to the brain of an illiterate person, the literate brain is massively changed. Once children learn to read, their brains are literally different."

There are two other important aspects of Ehri's work that relate to OM: (1) ways we read words and (2) how children grow as readers—or, phases of reading development. These concepts help explain why memorization of words simply isn't sustainable, and they help us identify appropriate instructional strategies to use for various stages of reading development.

In What Ways Do We Typically Read Words?

According to Ehri, these are the strategies we use to read unfamiliar words, ranked from least reliable to most reliable (2000, 2005, 2014, 2022, 2023):

LEAST RELIABLE

1. **Prediction:** Using context clues and some initial cues (such as first letters), we can predict what a word might be. This simply isn't reliable! Even if there had been a picture of *slough* in Molly's murder mystery, prediction, using the first letter, probably would not have prompted her to guess *slough*.

2. **Analogy:** Often, if we can read one word (e.g., *table*), we can read another word with the same or a similar part (e.g., *gable*). While helpful at times, analogy has its limits. Remember *slough*—and all the sounds *ough* makes? Reading from analogy didn't help Molly!

3. **Decoding:** We can use letter-sound knowledge to break a word apart, hold individual sounds briefly in memory (e.g., /p/ /l/ /ay/), and then blend them to decode the word (e.g., *play*). As we explain in the next chapter, the vast majority of words are decodable.

4. **Memory/Sight:** When we see a word, we automatically retrieve it from long-term memory. In other words, when we see the spelling of a word, our brain automatically retrieves that word's pronunciation. This is the most reliable and efficient strategy.

MOST RELIABLE

Just to drive the point home, it is not reliable to predict or guess words as texts become more complex and pictures go away. Also, our ability to make analogies is limited as we encounter more complex and lower frequency words. While decoding requires a lot of effort, it is the most effective way to ensure that a word's pronunciation aligns with its spelling, which, as you'll recall, is the glue to store the word in memory so that it can eventually be read automatically by sight.

Skills Necessary for OM

What skills do students need to decode, which leads to the ability to read words automatically? Thankfully, Ehri (1998, 2005, 2014; Miles & Ehri, 2019) has us covered here, as well. She explains that students need:

- phoneme segmentation skills, or the ability to segment spoken words into their smallest sound units (*rain* contains three phonemes: /r/ /ai/ /n/).
- grapheme-phoneme correspondence knowledge, or the knowledge of the letter-sound units in the writing system (/r/ is spelled with an *r*; /ā/ can be spelled *a_e*, *ai*, *ay*, and in many other ways!; /n/ is spelled with an *n*).
- opportunities to practice orthographically mapping the word, or repeated opportunities to analyze the letter-sound relationships within particular words (*rain* is spelled with *ai*, not *a_e*).
- knowledge of word meaning, or the opportunity to connect the meaning of the word to its spelling and pronunciation (*rain* is water that falls in drops from the sky).

Quantity and Quality of Exposures Matter

Readers need multiple exposures to learn words! The number of exposures that students need to "learn a word" varies by skill level and by the type of word (Steacy et al., 2020):

- Reitsma (1983) found that students needed to see and read printed words 1 to 4 times before they are permanently stored as sight words (as cited in Kilpatrick, 2015).
- Ehri and Saltmarsh (1995) showed that it took 4.4 exposures for higher performing readers to learn nonwords, but 9.3 exposures for lower performing readers.
- Stuart et al. (2000) found, when using flash cards to introduce five-year olds to eight new words, that after 32 exposures, only 60 percent of the students learned all eight words!
- Steacy and colleagues (2020) found that average first-grade, at-risk students required 5.65 exposures to the word, but low performing first-grade, at-risk students required 6.32 exposures to the word.

Keep in mind, though, it's not just the quantity of exposures that matters, but also the quality! Those exposures must include phoneme segmentation, letter-sound knowledge, word analysis, and meaning. That may help explain the frustration you feel when you've taught a word 25 times, and the student still can't read it!

How Do Children Grow as Word Readers and Spellers?

You're probably starting to see that getting words into long-term memory is complicated. Yet Ehri's research helps us understand the developmental process that students move through to do that. Ehri (2000, 2005, 2014, 2022, 2023) intentionally refers to points in that process as *phases* and not *stages*. Phases suggest fluidity and overlap, unlike stages, which suggest a more rigid and lockstep progression. Once you understand the phase a reader is in, you're better able to select from the instructional strategies we provide in later chapters.

Pre-Alphabetic Phase

Students begin their reading development in the pre-alphabetic phase, where they don't use letter-sound connections. Instead, they rely on visual cues, such as the arches in the McDonald's sign, the shape and color of a stop sign, or the logo on a tube of toothpaste. See page 51 for more on the pre-alphabetic reader.

Partial-Alphabetic Phase

As students learn letter-sound relationships, they begin to use some of this knowledge to read and spell words. In this partial-alphabetic phase, students may use their knowledge of the sound the first letter makes in a word to guess at the pronunciation of a word, and they may use the first and a middle or last sound to represent the spelling of a word. Don't be surprised if students remain in this phase for a while as they develop their ability to segment and blend phonemes and represent each phoneme in a word's spelling. Many older striving readers wind up stuck at an advanced level of this phase; they need explicit and systematic instruction in segmenting and blending sounds and overall letter-sound unit instruction to make forward progress. See page 52 for more on the partial-alphabetic reader.

Full-Alphabetic Phase

Once students apply their letter-sound knowledge to read complete words and represent all of the sounds in the words when spelling, they move into the full-alphabetic phase. Though they may be able to read groups of words, they might not accurately spell them. Students are in the full-alphabetic phase when they can segment all the sounds in a word and reasonably represent them with a letter or letter unit, even if it's not accurate. See page 85 for more on the full-alphabetic reader.

Consolidated Alphabetic Phase

Eventually, students move into the consolidated alphabetic phase when they are reading and spelling words accurately, using their knowledge of simple and complex grapheme-phoneme units, syllables, prefixes, roots, and suffixes (Ehri, 2000, 2005, 2014, 2022, 2023). See page 117 for more on consolidated alphabetic readers.

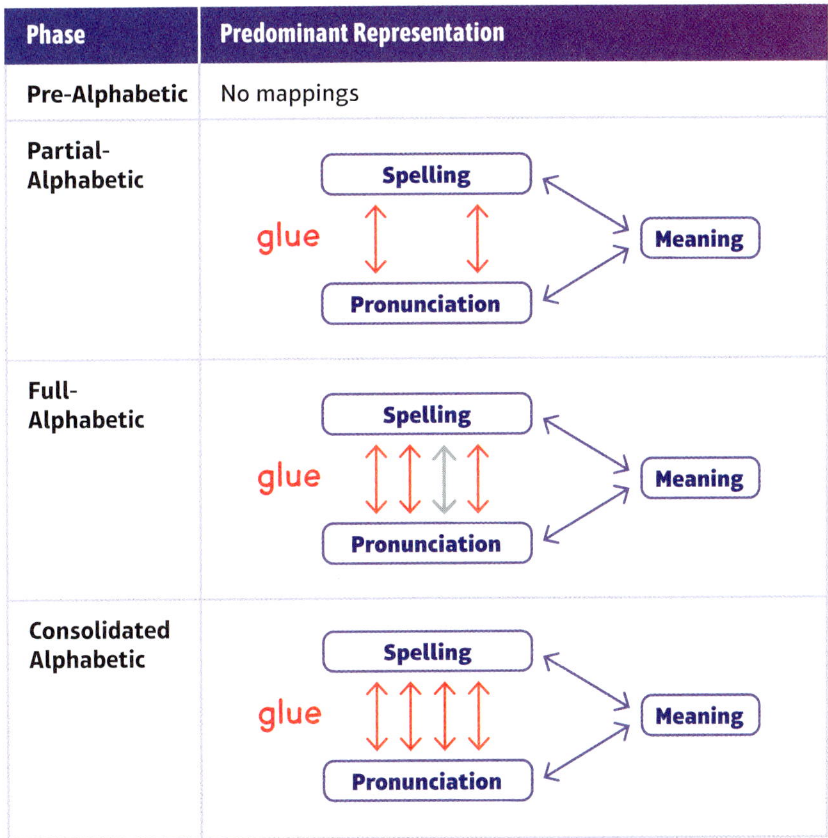

Phase	Predominant Representation
Pre-Alphabetic	No mappings
Partial-Alphabetic	
Full-Alphabetic	
Consolidated Alphabetic	

(Miles & Ehri, 2019)

Note that the gray arrow in the above chart represents an inaccurate grapheme representation but an attempt to represent the phoneme.

In Closing, Remember...

Orthographic mapping is the key to proficient reading.

- It enables students to read words by sight so that mental energy can be put toward comprehension.
- When readers don't automatically recognize words, they expend their precious cognitive energy on lifting words off the page. Decoding becomes laborious, and fluency slows, and that mental exertion takes a toll on their comprehension.
- The more we power up our students' orthographic mapping, the more we increase their ability to understand what they read.

Next, we explore the most coveted and often misunderstood category of words used in classrooms—high-frequency words—and the conditions necessary to make them stick in memory.

Terms to Remember	
Continuous Text	A piece of writing that is structured by compiling sentences into paragraphs, and, for books, sections, chapters, and parts.
Ehri's Phases of Reading	**Pre-alphabetic:** Children in this phase do not use alphabetic knowledge to read or spell words and instead rely on visual cues. **Partial-alphabetic:** Children in the partial-alphabetic phase demonstrate emerging use of grapheme phoneme, or letter-sound correspondences, by using incomplete connections to read and spell words. **Full-alphabetic:** In the full-alphabetic phase, students read and spell words by attending to most of the letter-sound correspondences, but often their pronunciation and/or spelling is an approximation, not fully accurate. **Consolidated alphabetic:** Readers in this phase begin to use chunks of words to decode, rather than individual letter-sound relationships. Multi-letter patterns—such as consonant blends, digraphs, vowel teams—as well as common syllables, affixes, and base words are consolidated in memory and recognized instantly.
Emergent Readers	Students who are at the beginning of their development of reading, as evidenced by showing some basic foundation literacy skills.
Fluency	The ability to speak, read, or write a language easily and effortlessly, almost as in a conversational tone.
fMRI	A noninvasive brain imaging technique that measures brain activity by tracking blood flow in the brain. This has been used to help detect specifically how brains read.
Frontal Lobe (Broca's Area)	The part of the brain that plans and produces speech and processes grammar and morphology.
Grapheme	A unit of a writing system, such as a letter or digraph.
Grapheme-Phoneme Connection (GPC)	The correspondences between the units of sound within a word and the grapheme (written unit) that represents that sound.
Linguistic Knowledge	The knowledge of a language that allows people to use and understand it.

Terms to Remember cont.	
Neuroplasticity	The brain's ability to change and adapt its structure and function. This process can occur in response to internal or external stimuli, such as learning a new skill or recovering from an injury.
Occipital Lobe (Visual Word Form Area)	The part of the brain that can detect and process the shapes and visual features of letters.
Parietal Lobe (Angular Gyrus)	The part of the brain responsible for grapheme-phoneme conversion.
Phoneme	The smallest unit of sound within a language system. A phoneme may be a word by itself, or it may be combined with other phonemes to make a word.
Phoneme Segmentation	The ability to break down a spoken word into its individual sounds, or phonemes, which is a crucial skill for developing reading and spelling abilities, as it involves identifying and separating each distinct sound within a word.
Reading Brain/ Reading Circuit	The parts of the brain that work together to help us make sense of the words we read: • The visual cortex that helps perceive words. • The phonological cortex that maps the sounds to letters. • The semantic cortex that stores word meaning. • The syntactic cortex that helps us understand the rules and structures of sentences.
Semantics/Semantic Relations	The study of the meanings of words.
Striving Readers	Students who are experiencing challenges with reading and may need help catching up to meet grade-level expectations.
Temporal Lobe (Wernicke's Area)	The part of the brain that helps with syntax and meaning.
Visual Processing	The brain's ability to interpret and use visual information from the world around us.

CHAPTER 2

The Lowdown on High-Frequency Words

Remember Katie's story from her early days of teaching? How she encouraged her students to memorize word lists? She was operating on the common misconception that the most commonly used words in English are so irregular that they need to be memorized. Even then she wondered if there was a better approach. Which phonetic concepts should she teach? Do rules such as "When two vowels go walking, the first one does the talking" apply to most words? Should she have students memorize words? And what about really wonky words with uncommon spelling patterns, such as *choir* and *would*? How frequently are those words used in the emergent reading years? A self-professed reading geek, Katie was determined to figure all of that out.

Understanding the Many Categories of Words

You might be surprised by all the ways words can be categorized: high-frequency and low-frequency words, content and function words, regularly and irregularly spelled words, real words and nonsense words, decodable words and sight words... oh, my!

In Chapter 1, we walked you through mapping one low-frequency word, *slough*, in memory. In this chapter, we dive into the most coveted category of words used in classrooms—high-frequency words—and the conditions necessary to make them stick in memory. By the end of the chapter, you'll understand why memorizing words as whole units is a flawed approach. You'll also think critically about whether high-frequency words are really all that irregular.

What's the Difference Between High-Frequency Words and Sight Words?

First, let's distinguish between high-frequency words and sight words. High-frequency words are those that appear most commonly in texts students read, typically making up 50 to 80 percent of those texts.

Watch Katie explain how high-frequency words work.

Interestingly, Green, Keogh, and Prout (2024) call into question the rigor and the relevance of the most widely used high-frequency word lists, such as the Dolch List and the Fry List, and instead offer a curated list of words from the most commonly used children's picture books. See their list on page 31.

Regardless of the list you're using, high-frequency words are simply words that are used a lot in text!

In Chapter 1, we drove the point home that any word becomes a sight word after it has been orthographically mapped in memory through analysis of its spelling, pronunciation, and meaning. Words that a student automatically retrieves from memory, or reads instantly, are sight words. So, after enough exposures, both the low-frequency word *slough* and the high-frequency word *the* become sight words!

Common Names for High-Frequency Words

- Dolch Words
- Fry Words
- Snap Words
- Flash Words
- Popcorn Words
- Power Words
- Heart Words
- Need-to-Know Words
- Word-Wall Words

The First 100 Children's Picture Book (CPB) Sight Words							
1	the	26	at	51	little	76	their
2	and	27	are	52	time	77	could
3	a	28	one	53	from	78	about
4	to	29	said	54	had	79	back
5	I	30	what	55	now	80	who
6	you	31	this	56	will	81	or
7	in	32	when	57	I'm	82	make
8	of	33	we	58	go	83	into
9	it	34	me	59	were	84	look
10	he	35	have	60	too	85	very
11	is	36	as	61	them	86	would
12	was	37	do	62	him	87	right
13	for	38	like	63	some	88	here
14	on	39	out	64	big	89	love
15	that	40	can	65	get	90	way
16	with	41	her	66	if	91	night
17	but	42	not	67	good	92	did
18	his	43	then	68	don't	93	new
19	all	44	your	69	down	94	come
20	they	45	no	70	by	95	our
21	my	46	there	71	how	96	two
22	so	47	day	72	know	97	want
23	be	48	just	73	an	98	made
24	she	49	it's	74	oh	99	over
25	up	50	see	75	more	100	around

(Green et al., 2024)

Download the First 100 Children's Picture Book (CPB) Sight Words.

Remember, the goal for students is for *all* words to become sight words. Although categories of low-frequency words and high-frequency words will not change, whether a word is a sight word for a student *will* change as learning occurs. We want as many words as possible stored securely so that students can read them automatically. Therefore, our objective for early reading instruction should focus on storing as many words as possible in long-term memory.

A great way to accelerate early readers' ability to map high-frequency words and apply their newly learned phonics knowledge is to give them decodable texts, meaning texts that contain words that align to students' level of phonics knowledge and reflect a solid phonics scope and sequence (see examples below). As students read decodable text, we encourage them to apply their letter-sound skills to read the words. They glue the spelling and the pronunciation of the word together as they come to understand the word's meaning through its context and usage. This is a great way to turn words into sight words!

These days, high-quality decodable texts come in a variety of formats and genres for many grade levels.

Let's be clear: Decodable passages will have lots of regularly spelled (decodable) high-frequency words (e.g., *if*, *with*, *cat*, *man*), and they may have a limited number of irregularly spelled (not decodable) high-frequency words (e.g., *of*, *the*, *are*). This is where the definition of high-frequency words depends on whether you are referring to a limited list of specific words your students use or to higher-frequency words that commonly occur in text but aren't part of a list. *Cat* may not be on your word list, for example, but it is certainly a common word in texts for emergent readers.

There's a misconception that high-frequency words are so irregular that they simply need to be memorized as whole units. The remainder of this chapter explores how high-frequency words work so that you have the knowledge you need to help students better store these words in memory—the way their brains work best.

Are Most High-Frequency Words Really Irregular?

Let's investigate a career-defining point in Katie's early teaching: the notion that high-frequency words are so irregular that they simply must be memorized. As she and her colleagues wrote in *The Reading Teacher*,

> The belief that words on high-frequency/sight-word lists are irregularly spelled and thus impossible or inadvisable to decode remains a prevalent mind-set. Although this may be true for some words, it is certainly not the case for the majority (2017).

Katie and her colleagues, Denise Eide and Janee' Butler (2024), analyzed the Dolch List of 220 high-frequency words. They applied 75 phonetics rules (letter-sound correspondence) and 31 spelling rules to the words, and found that 99 percent of them followed those rules. In other words, 99 percent of the Dolch List are regularly spelled or decodable!

Beware of Function Words!

Ever played Charades? Remember "little words," such as *of*, *for*, *this*, *was*, *that*, *with*, *from*, *by*? High-frequency word lists are full of function words, which serve a grammatical function but typically don't have a clear-cut definition. For instance, how would you define *which* or *their*? The meanings of these words are contained in their use in a sentence, or the syntactical structure of the sentence.

Emergent readers, including multilingual students learning to read in English, need to use function words in meaningful sentences in order to understand their syntactic use in context. Our routine—described in Chapter 3—includes specific ways to approach those pesky function words.

Making High-Frequency Words Stick

Well, then, you may ask, what is the best approach for getting high-frequency words to stick in memory? First, students need to have enough foundational skills to even deal with these words. Katie and her colleagues, Karen McFadden and Linnea Ehri (2018), found that kindergarteners in the partial-alphabetic phase—the phase in which students are beginning to use letter-sound correspondences but cannot yet fully decode—couldn't learn a certain set of words from a high-frequency list on flash cards at the same rate as their classmates in the full-alphabetic phase, even though the words were presented to them in the same way for the equivalent number of exposures. Students in the partial-alphabetic phase would benefit more from working on their phonemic awareness, letter-sound knowledge, and basic decoding skills rather than learning high-frequency words in isolation.

Sorting Words for Your Grade Level

Here's what you need to know to sort your high-frequency words for your grade level:

- What letter-sound knowledge do your students have right now?
- What letter-sound knowledge will your students learn at some point this year?
- What letter-sound knowledge is not covered by your instructional materials and/or phonics scope and sequence?

We encourage you to collaborate with grade-based colleagues to sort your words.

Research suggests that the best way to get higher-frequency words into memory is to have students decode them (Miles et al., 2024)! Let's examine a few examples from the Dolch List (1936): *but*, *had*, *not*. These three words are all simple CVC words, with short medial vowel sounds. There's no need for students to memorize those words because they can simply decode them. When students decode a word, they make connections between the word's spelling and pronunciation; this serves as the glue to make words stick in memory (Ehri, 2022). After students decode these words, they reinforce them in decodable text.

But what about high-frequency words that contain letter-sound relationships or spelling patterns that you aren't going to teach? You can rely on your phonics scope and sequence to sort the words into three categories, according to decodability (Miles et al., 2017; 2024): (1) regularly spelled, (2) temporarily irregularly spelled, and (3) permanently irregularly spelled.

- **Regularly spelled words** have common letter-sound correspondences that the student knows and can apply to read or spell.

- **Temporarily irregularly spelled words** have letter-sound correspondences that the student hasn't learned yet, but once they do, they will be able to apply the concept to read and spell. In the chart below, *eight* is temporarily irregular for students at the start of grade 2, when most scope and sequences have not yet covered the less common long-*a* pattern of *eigh*. But when students have had that feature explicitly taught, *eight* moves from temporarily irregular to regularly spelled.
- **Permanently irregularly spelled words** have letter-sound correspondences that are idiosyncratic to that word or only a few others. They may have silent letters or a common letter unit (e.g., *ai*) that is making an uncommon sound (e.g., /ĕ/).

How Do I Know if a Word Is Regular, Temporarily Irregular, or Permanently Irregular?

Does the student know the phonetic/linguistic concepts in the word?

- If **YES**, it's **regularly spelled**.
- If **NO**, ask: Are the phonetic concepts in the word on the school's phonics scope and sequence, meaning will it be taught in the upcoming lessons or grades?
    - If **YES**, the word is **temporarily irregularly spelled**.
    - If **NO**, the word is **irregularly spelled**.

Category	Definition	Example
Regularly spelled	Follow the conventions of the most common grapheme-phoneme relations	*can, flat, stripe*
Temporarily irregularly spelled	Require knowledge of grapheme-phoneme relations that students have not yet learned	*special*: learn the *cial* spelling/morphological unit *eight*: learn *eigh* says /ai/
Permanently irregularly spelled	Contain spelling patterns that are idiosyncratic to that word; may contain silent letters	*said*: /s/ /e/ /d/, *ai* says /e/ *were*: /w/ /er/, *ere* says /er/

(Miles et al., 2017; 2024)

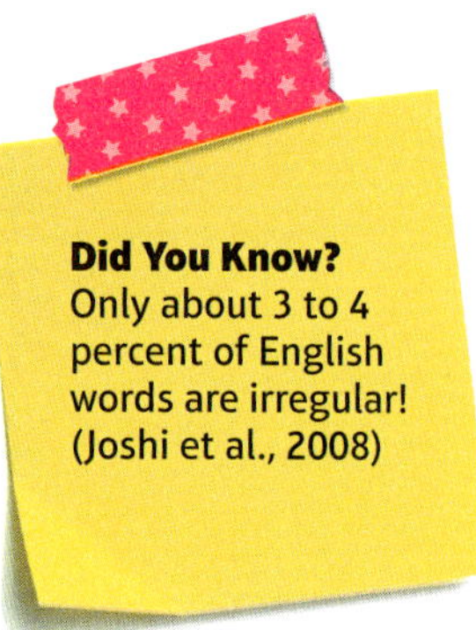

Teaching Permanently Irregular Words

Finally, let's discuss the most difficult category of words: permanently irregularly spelled words. We refer to them below as "irregular words."

Irregular words contain a spelling pattern that is unique to the word or a small group of words. They might contain a silent letter, or they might contain phoneme-grapheme units that don't follow their usual pattern (Miles et al., 2017; 2024). Early readers often encounter these irregular words: *of*, *one*, *said*, *been*, *again*, and *any/many*. What makes these words irregular? The table below provides that analysis:

The Permanently Irregular Word	The Linguistic Features That Don't Follow the Usual Phoneme-Grapheme Correspondence
of	*o* saying /u/ *f* saying /v/
one	*o* saying /w/, the *e* at the end suggests a *v_e* pattern
said	*ai* saying /e/
been	*ee* saying /e/
again	*ai* saying /e/
any/many	*a* saying /e/

Examples of high-frequency irregular words with silent letters include:

- *island*: silent *s*
- *people*: silent *o*
- *scissors*: silent *c*
- *Wednesday*: silent *d* and middle silent *e*

Decode Reliable Parts and Discuss "Yet-to-Be-Learned" Parts

Like temporarily irregular words, permanently irregular words contain many reliable letter-sound units that should be used to anchor the word in memory. In *island*, *people*, and *scissors*, for example, there is only one letter that is tricky or needs to be remembered. You can acknowledge the silent letter while students decode all the other letter-sound units. Here is an example of what you might say to a group of third graders about the word *people*:

people

"Let's sound out this word together (point to each letter-sound unit as you say it: /p/ /ē/ /p/ /l/). I don't hear any sound for the letter *o*, and I know that *eo* is not a common vowel unit. In this word, the *o* is silent" (underline, highlight, or box it).

Research-Based Ways to Help Students Learn Irregular Words

- Murray and colleagues (2019) suggest having kindergarten and first-grade students analyze words and draw a box around their irregular parts.
- Colenbrander and colleagues (2022) found two approaches to be more effective than reading words on flash cards: 1) Simply allow students to practice spelling the words. 2) Have students adjust their mispronunciation of a word they decode (e.g., /man/ /y/) to match a pronunciation of a word they know (e.g., /men/ /y/).

Those approaches are highly effective because they focus students' attention on the regular and irregular parts of words

In Closing, Remember...

- The vast majority of words in the English language are decodable.
- All words, including high-frequency words, become sight words through the process of orthographic mapping.
- High-frequency words appear most commonly in text.
- Function words hold semantic space, and are critical to the structure of English language, but they are difficult to define.
- Flash card drills, or basic memorization approaches, are not an efficient strategy for most students to make words stick.
- Draw students' attention to the spelling anomalies in irregular words, a process called "mental marking" (Murray et al., 2019).

Next, we explore our four-step instructional routine to help make words stick for students.

Terms to Remember	
Decodable Texts	Texts that contain words that align to students' level of phonics knowledge and progression along a phonics scope and sequence.
Dolch List	A list of frequently used English words compiled by Edward William Dolch, a major proponent of the "whole-word" method of early reading instruction, in 1936.
Fry List	A list of the most common words in English, organized by frequency. Edward Fry developed the list in the 1950s and updated it in 1980.
Function Words	Words that serve a grammatical function but typically don't have a clear-cut definition. For instance, how would you define *which* or *was*? Young readers have a harder time learning to read, spell, and use these words in sentences.
High-Frequency Words	The most frequently used words in written English. They make up 50 to 80 percent of the texts children are exposed to on a daily basis. There are three types of high-frequency words: **Regularly Spelled:** Words that have common letter-sound correspondences that students have learned and can apply when reading or spelling. In other words, decodable words that follow phonics rules, such as *and*, *but*, and *see*. **Temporarily Irregularly Spelled:** Words that have letter-sound correspondences that students haven't learned yet, but once they do, they will be able to apply them when reading or spelling. **Permanently Irregularly Spelled:** Words that have letter-sound correspondences that are idiosyncratic to that word or only a few others.
Letter-Sound Correspondence	The relationship between written letters (graphemes) and the sounds (phonemes) they represent.
Medial	The "middle sound" of a CVC word—the vowel sound.
Sight Words	Words that can be recognized immediately, or "by sight," without having to sound out the letters.

CHAPTER 3

An Instructional Routine for Making Words Stick

By now, we hope you have an understanding of the what and the why of orthographic mapping to support students' reading development. In this chapter, we get into the how: our four-part instructional routine.

An Overview of Our Routine

So how do we take evidence-based theories that explain how we read words and that explain what happens in our brains when we read words and apply them to daily practice? Well, we've devised a routine. The goal of the routine is to maximize students' opportunities to identify and spell words so that eventually they will instantly and effortlessly recognize the word and transfer this knowledge to many reading and writing contexts. While our routine is grounded in research and has been used in classrooms, we are hard at work investigating its effectiveness.

Furthermore, our routine is designed to work with and for all learners. We are particularly cognizant of the literacy needs of children from diverse linguistic and dialectical backgrounds and children with neurodivergence that makes learning to read difficult. Our routine aligns with key principles of structured literacy and provides explicit teacher modeling and clear explanation. The activities we recommend build foundational skills, such as oral language, phonological awareness, and knowledge of sound-symbol correspondences.

Our routine follows four steps that align with what we've explained about powering up orthographic mapping thus far.

Step	Goal
1 See & Say	Students see the word and then make a phonological representation of the word in order to access the word's sound structure. Simply put, they hear the word and say the word aloud while looking at it.
2 Segment & Spell	Students identify the word's grapheme-phoneme correspondences by mapping the word's sounds to its letters.
3 Study & Suss Out	Students explore the meaning of the word and its usage. They understand multiple meanings of the word, as well as the various ways the word is used in sentences.
4 Search & Stick	Students move toward automatically recognizing and retrieving the word when it appears in text.

Research That Informs Our Routine

Literacy development is so vital to children's health, education, career trajectory, and lifelong success that the United States government has commissioned and funded reports to synthesize research findings (*Becoming a Nation of Readers*, 1985; *Report of the National Reading Panel*, 2000). Based on those reports, and more recent research findings, the Institute of Education Sciences developed practice guides to support educators with translating research into practice. Two of those guides support the process of orthographic mapping by decoding and encoding words: *Foundational Skills to Support Reading for Understanding in Kindergarten Through 3rd Grade* (Foorman et al., 2016) and *Providing Reading Interventions for Students in Grades 4–9* (Vaughn et al., 2022). We've drawn the following recommendations from those guides and discuss how they apply to our instructional routine.

1 Develop awareness of the segments of sounds in speech and how they link to letters (Foorman et al., 2016).

It's no surprise that students must be taught to recognize and manipulate sounds in words and link those sounds to letters. In our routine, we provide multiple ways to build the grapheme-phoneme correspondences that are essential to reading and spelling.

2 Teach students to decode words, analyze word parts, and write and recognize words (Foorman et al., 2016).

The focus here is on enhancing students' blending skills, as well as the connection between reading words and spelling them. As you'll soon see, our routine does not apply only to decoding—or lifting words off the page—but also to encoding, or spelling. We provide explicit instruction in spelling words, at the letter-sound level and through the recognition of word parts and the study of morphology.

3 Build students' decoding skills to read complex multisyllabic words (Vaughn et al., 2022).

The need to build students' decoding and encoding skills does not end in second grade! In fact, for students to become fluent readers, they need strategic approaches to read and spell the multisyllabic words that they encounter in upper-elementary and secondary classrooms. In applying our routine to upper-elementary students, we are intentional about teaching meaning chunks—or morphemes—in words, which helps students be strategic in approaching multisyllabic words.

4 Provide purposeful fluency-building activities to help students read effortlessly (Vaughn et al., 2022).

Remembering that fluency is essential to comprehension, we are mindful that the intent of orthographic mapping is efficient and accurate word recognition. As the What Works Clearinghouse guide reminds us, "When students read fluently, they can turn their attention from sounding out the individual words to making sense of what they are reading" (Vaughn et al., 2022). Hence, the final step of our routine provides accuracy and automaticity practice, which is essential to becoming a fluent reader.

Step 1: See & Say

First, we present children with the orthographic representation of the word. This just means we show them the word and point to its spelling. By doing that, we activate the occipital lobe of students' brains—the portion largely responsible for visual processing and scanning letter shapes (Wolf, 2008). We might show students the word in multiple forms—handwritten, lowercase, uppercase first letter, typed out in various fonts, and even cursive (where relevant). Doing this reminds students that a word is the same word, regardless of its appearance.

A Glimpse of Step 1 in Action

See & Say: *bath*

Show students the word and have them say it aloud with you. "The word is *bath*. Say it with me."

Children not only see the word, they say it. By doing that, they create a phonological representation of the word. Hearing a word's pronunciation is a crucial step in identifying that word (Ehri, 2005). In *Brain Words*, Richard Gentry and Gene Ouellette (2025) explain that having students listen to and say the word requires auditory analysis and phonological working memory. The first step in our protocol gives students "auditory bombardment" (Gentry & Ouellette, 2025), flooding the brain circuitry with the sound-processing elements. Saying the word activates the brain's frontal and temporal lobes, helping students understand the word's sound structure.

Step 2: Segment & Spell

Next, students explore the word's linguistic structure by linking its phonemes to its graphemes. We start by identifying the sequence of phonemes in the word, guiding students to divide the word's sounds at various levels: the syllable level, the onset-rime level, and the individual phoneme level.

Did You Know?
Researchers have found that visual memory for letter strings is limited to two or three letters max! (Aaron et al., 1998) More evidence that rote memorization is not effective!

In this step of the routine, we identify parts of the word that are phonetically regular, based on the concepts students have learned thus far, and parts that are not regular (as we explored in Chapter 2!). Students must understand how a particular sound in a word maps to a letter or letter combination. For instance, in the word *they*, we discuss that the /th/ sound is spelled *th*, and the long /a/ sound is spelled *ey*. Notice that we are not encouraging students to memorize the spelling of the word, as studies indicated that visual memory is not actually a key to good spelling (Cassar et al., 2005).

A Glimpse of Step 2 in Action

Segment & Spell: *bath*

- Break *bath* into onset and rime: /b/ /ath/.
- Next, have students break *bath* into three phonemes: /b/ /a/ /th/.
- Point out that the /th/ is a digraph, or two letters making one sound.

Breaking a Word Into Various Levels

- The syllable level: /stick/
- The onset-rime level: /st/ /ick/
- The individual phoneme level: /s/ /t/ /i/ /k/

Step 3: Study & Suss Out

While the first two steps might capture what you're already doing in your phonics instruction, we often gloss over morphology exploration. Because we need the meaning of a word to orthographically map it, here we lead conversations about the meaning of the word and use illustrations to enhance understanding. By studying the meaning of the word and sussing it out, children activate the areas of the brain dealing with language comprehension and word meaning.

The Fuss About *Suss*

Haven't heard of the British word *suss*, or haven't heard it in a while? Molly first encountered it as a teenager in The Who's rock opera *Tommy*, when a character claims he needs to "suss everything out." The *Cambridge Dictionary* defines it as "to realize, understand, or discover something." Gobsmacked by this powerful new word, Molly immediately used it as much as possible (much to the annoyance of her older brother). She watched as Jessica Fletcher sussed out the killer in the beloved 1980s mystery series *Murder, She Wrote*. She sussed out the proofs in her algebra homework. You get the picture.

Our aim here is to build students' understandings of the word's meaning by discussing semantic networks and appropriate usage and application of the word. For instance, if students encounter the word *cat*, certain features immediately jump to mind: whiskers, tail, ears, etc. Other associated semantic features might also pop up: famous cats (e.g., Garfield), behaviors of cats (chasing mice), or traits of cats (lapping up a bowl of milk). All of these semantic features assist in our ability to recognize the word, apply it to context, and use it appropriately. When children see a word, they are better able to remember phonological and semantic information than when words are taught without their orthographic forms (Chambré et al., 2017; Miles & Ehri, 2019; Ricketts et al., 2009; Rosenthal & Ehri, 2008).

To ensure correct use of the word in speaking and writing, and comprehension of the word in reading and listening, we provide contexts of the word, discuss the word's multiple meanings, and examine examples and non-examples of the word. At the end of this step, we incorporate the word's meaning and appropriate semantic usage. After all, what good is being able to segment, say, and spell a word if you don't know how to use it in speaking and writing?

A Glimpse of Step 3 in Action

Study & Suss Out: *bath*

- Explain that a bath is a way to get clean by immersing ourself in water.
- Use the word in context, as in "Do you take a bath or a shower at your house?"
- Generate words associated with *bath*: *bathtub*, *soak*, *clean*, *bubble bath*, *bathroom*, etc. Show a picture of a bath.

Step 4: Search & Stick

The last step in our routine increases the automaticity with which students recognize words in isolation and those same words in texts. Our aim as teachers should be to develop in our students the ability to extend what they have learned in one context to new contexts (Bransford et al., 1999). This step is designed to help students connect decoding and encoding to text, thereby increasing the likelihood of transfer.

In the final step, we provide automaticity practice to increase students' word recognition. We might lead students on "word hunts," in which they search texts for the target words or words with similar linguistic features. We move decoding and encoding instruction out of isolation by connecting them to text. It may seem obvious, but the intention of word identification and spelling is to unlock students' ability to read and write different kinds of text—decodable and authentic. Additionally, we build accuracy so that word identification and spelling are fluent and effortless.

A Glimpse of Step 4 in Action

Search & Stick: *bath*

- Connect a linguistic feature of the word, such as the ending /th/, to decodable text and/or authentic text—for instance, the decodable text *This Moth*.
- Consider sending students on a word hunt, where they search texts for words with similar linguistic features, such as the ending /th/.

The Menu of Activities for Grades K–5

When we have time, we love to partake in New York City's annual Restaurant Week. During it, restaurants offer a prix-fixe lunch at a vastly reduced cost. The menu is divided into its typical categories: appetizers, salads, entrees, and desserts, but the options are limited. To get the deal, you must order one item from each category—no substitutions!

Our instructional routine is like a prix-fixe meal; you must select one activity from each menu category to ensure students orthographically map words by analyzing their spelling, pronunciation, and meaning. Now, there's still choice, but like a prix-fixe menu, you must select an activity from each section of the routine.

We provide a rationale and overview for each activity, along with language you might use when carrying it out. Below are some points to keep in mind.

- This routine is best used during small-group instruction.
- Select a set of target words based on the skill level of the students. A set of 3 to 4 words may be best for emergent readers, while a set of 6 to 7 words may be right for advanced readers.
- Be sure the phonetic pattern of the target words relate. For example, emergent readers may be working with *bat*, *cat*, *rat*, and *hat*, while advanced readers may be working with *bridge*, *ridge*, *hedge*, *lodge*, *badge*, *dodge*, and *grudge*.
- Take each word through all four steps of the routine.
- Tweak the language to meet your students' needs and your style.
- Use the instructional materials you likely already have on hand, such as student whiteboards, magnetic letters, and stopwatches, and feel free to replace what we suggest. For example, if an activity calls for magnetic letters and you only have letter tiles, use tiles!
- Keep in mind the "why" of each activity, as well as the "what" and "how." We help you do that by citing a bit of research within activities.

The Menu of Activities

Grades	See & Say	Segment & Spell	Study & Suss Out	Search & Stick
K–1	• See It, Call It • See It, Say It, Sing It/Shout It/ Robot It • See It, Say It, Mirror It • See It, Say It, Jump It	• Tap It, Spell It • Count It, Map It • Word Chain It • March It, Spell It • Tap It, Unscramble It	• Sketch It • Act It Out • Picture It • Check Its Use • Know Its Many Meanings • Word Parts **Function Words:** • Hear It, Use It • Choose It, Use It	• Sort It • Swat It • Hunt for It
2–3	• See It, Say It, Slide It • See It, Say It, Clap It • See It, Say It, Chin It • See It in Different Ways, Say It	• Count It, Box It, Spell It • Count It, Spell It Three Ways • Count It, Line It, Spell It	• Word Web It • Word Expert Card It • Paint Swatch It • Word Parts • Know Its Many Meanings • Word Ladder It **Function Words:** • Hear It, Use It • Choose It, Use It	• Hunt for It • Word Sorts • Find Its Look- Alike
4–5	• See It, Say It, Scoop It • See It, Say It, Highlight It	• Count It, Cover It, Chunk Spell It, Check It • Count It, Box It	• Study Its Root • Frayer Model It **Function Words:** • Hear It, Use It • Choose It, Use It	• Word Part Chart It • Build It • Hunt for It

Choosing Words for Activities

We designed the routine to align with a wide variety of instructional materials and curricular programs, allowing you to adapt it to your program's scope and sequence. When considering words to use in activities, we encourage you to choose them based on where your students are on your program's scope and sequence. If you don't have a scope and sequence—or you're not satisfied with the one you do have—we recommend the one designed for Scholastic's Ready4Reading™ program.

We encourage you to consider the phonetic concepts that you have taught or are teaching from your phonics scope and sequence. Then consider words you are asking students to read and spell. It just makes good sense to have students read and spell words that contain the letter-sound correspondences you have taught or are teaching. It's like giving students more swings at bat! Emergent readers need a lot of practice connecting concepts from the scope and sequence, and many opportunities to analyze and read words that contain those concepts, in isolation and in context. They also need to write words that

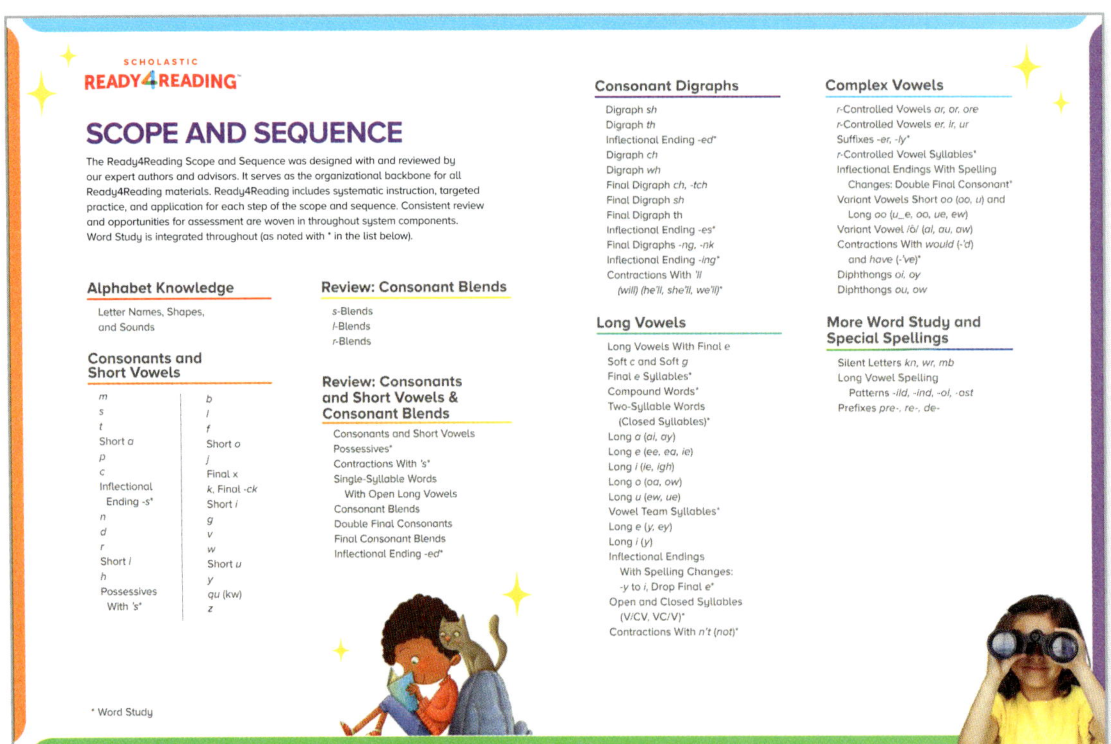

SCHOLASTIC READY4READING™

SCOPE AND SEQUENCE

The Ready4Reading Scope and Sequence was designed with and reviewed by our expert authors and advisors. It serves as the organizational backbone for all Ready4Reading materials. Ready4Reading includes systematic instruction, targeted practice, and application for each step of the scope and sequence. Consistent review and opportunities for assessment are woven in throughout system components. Word Study is integrated throughout (as noted with * in the list below).

Alphabet Knowledge

Letter Names, Shapes, and Sounds

Consonants and Short Vowels

m
s
t
Short *a*
p
c
Inflectional Ending *-s**
n
d
r
Short *i*
h
Possessives With *'s**
b
l
f
Short *o*
j
Final x
k, Final *-ck*
Short *i*
g
v
w
Short *u*
y
qu (kw)
z

Review: Consonant Blends

s-Blends
l-Blends
r-Blends

Review: Consonants and Short Vowels & Consonant Blends

Consonants and Short Vowels
Possessives*
Contractions With *'s**
Single-Syllable Words With Open Long Vowels
Consonant Blends
Double Final Consonants
Final Consonant Blends
Inflectional Ending *-ed**

Consonant Digraphs

Digraph *sh*
Digraph *th*
Inflectional Ending *-ed**
Digraph *ch*
Digraph *wh*
Final Digraph *ch*, *-tch*
Final Digraph *sh*
Final Digraph th
Inflectional Ending *-es**
Final Digraphs *-ng*, *-nk*
Inflectional Ending *-ing**
Contractions With *'ll* *(will) (he'll, she'll, we'll)**

Long Vowels

Long Vowels With Final *e*
Soft *c* and Soft *g*
Final *e* Syllables*
Compound Words*
Two-Syllable Words (Closed Syllables)*
Long *a* (*ai*, *ay*)
Long *e* (*ee*, *ea*, *ie*)
Long *i* (*ie*, *igh*)
Long *o* (*oa*, *ow*)
Long *u* (*ew*, *ue*)
Vowel Team Syllables*
Long *e* (*y*, *ey*)
Long *i* (*y*)
Inflectional Endings With Spelling Changes: *-y* to *i*, Drop Final *e**
Open and Closed Syllables (V/CV, VC/V)*
Contractions With *n't* (*not*)*

Complex Vowels

r-Controlled Vowels *ar*, *or*, *ore*
r-Controlled Vowels *er*, *ir*, *ur*
Suffixes *-er*, *-ly**
r-Controlled Vowel Syllables*
Inflectional Endings With Spelling Changes: Double Final Consonant*
Variant Vowels Short *oo* (*oo*, *u*) and Long *oo* (*u_e*, *oo*, *ue*, *ew*)
Variant Vowel /ô/ (*al*, *au*, *aw*)
Contractions With *would* (-'*d*) and *have* (-'*ve*)*
Diphthongs *oi*, *oy*
Diphthongs *ou*, *ow*

More Word Study and Special Spellings

Silent Letters *kn*, *wr*, *mb*
Long Vowel Spelling Patterns *-ild*, *-ind*, *-ol*, *-ost*
Prefixes *pre-*, *re-*, *de-*

* Word Study

contain those concepts, in isolation and in context. Of course, a few other irregular high-frequency words that you have explicitly taught by analyzing the letter-sound anomalies should be included, too.

The crux of our routine is explicit word study. The English language is complex in etymology (the study of word's origins and evolutions), structure and usage, derivation and meaning, and linguistic features. Our routine offers opportunities for you and your students to engage in rich conversations about how words work. Word study—the amalgamation of analyzing a word's spelling, pronunciation, meaning, and usage—empowers readers to build a rich lexicon.

In Closing, Remember...

Our routine is based on important reviews of research on the best ways to help students learn to read and spell words (Foorman et al., 2016; Vaughn et al., 2022). It has four steps:

- Step 1: See & Say
- Step 2: Segment & Spell
- Step 3: Study & Suss Out
- Step 4: Search & Stick

In the next three chapters, we show you how to make words stick in grades K–1, 2–3, and 4–5. In each chapter, we offer a menu of activities for each step that will help you take students through a rigorous and engaging word-learning process.

As you implement those activities, be mindful that they might straddle more than one of the steps in our routine. Similarly, they might hit on more than one component of orthographic mapping: a word's visual representation, sound structure, and meaning. Try not to get caught up in this. Instead, keep your eyes on the prize of using systematic, easy-to-implement, and engaging ways to power up orthographic mapping.

Terms to Remember	
Authentic Texts	These books consider students' general reading development and select topics with real-world purposes. They are not controlled by phonics patterns. They are meant to be read independently or listened to and eventually read by students.
Automaticity	The ability to accurately and effortlessly recognize words. It's a fundamental skill that's part of reading fluency, which also includes speed, expression, and comprehension.
Decoding	The ability to translate a word from print to speech, or to identify a word from a string of letters. It's a key literacy skill that's taught as early as preschool and kindergarten and is the foundation for other reading skills like fluency, vocabulary, and comprehension.
Encoding	The translation of a spoken word or sound into print. This is what we refer to as spelling. When learning to encode, students must first know the alphabet and the sounds that letters make.
Etymology	The study of the origins of words and how their meanings have changed over time. It can be a valuable tool for literacy, helping students understand the building blocks of language and how words are formed and are related.
Explicit Word Study	A direct and intentional approach to teaching students about word patterns, sounds, and meanings. A teacher clearly explains and models concepts, providing specific examples and guided practice to ensure students fully understand each element of a word, rather than relying on implicit learning or guessing.
Lexicon	All the words a person knows. *Lexicon* is from the Greek word *lexikon* (*biblion*) meaning "word (book)."
Onset-Rime	The onset is the part of a single-syllable word before the vowel. The rime is the part of a word that includes the vowel and letters that follow. Examples: *b-ug, cl-ock, str-ipe.*
Semantics	The study of the meaning of words, phrases, and sentences in a language. It's a key component of reading comprehension and literacy, in general.

Making Words Stick in Grades K and 1

CHAPTER 4

Students in primary classrooms are like airplanes, gathering speed on the runway to take off into reading. All of their letter knowledge and phonemic awareness skills launch them into their initial ascent of word reading and spelling. Our kindergarten and first-grade classrooms are full of eager readers in pre- and partial-alphabetic phases.

Pre-Alphabetic Readers

Though they may be able to sing the alphabet song, pre-alphabetic readers have not yet mastered the alphabetic principle, or that written language is based on correspondences between letter names and their sounds (Ehri, 2000, 2005, 2014, 2022, 2023). Their ability to recognize words relies on visual cues (the colors and circle of the Target store sign, the shape of the STOP sign). As shown in Callie's writing sample at right, their writing is symbol salad—a combination of squiggles, letters, and letter-like approximations.

In addition to building oral language skills, instruction should focus on developing students' letter knowledge and phonological awareness. Because they are

The writing of a child in the pre-alphabetic phase of reading development

in such early stages of reading, students are still mastering foundational skills that will eventually support orthographic mapping, but they aren't yet using letters or phonemes in a strategic way to read or spell words.

Partial-Alphabetic Readers

Eventually, students leverage their phonemic awareness skills and letter knowledge to begin to read and spell words. In other words, they start moving toward the partial-alphabetic phase (Ehri, 2000, 2005, 2014, 2022, 2023). They may guess at a word by using their basic letter-sound knowledge and applying it to the first letter—or first few letters—in the word. For example, they may read *horse* as *house*. Sometimes, students may read words accurately by using initial letter-sound information and combining it with context clues or picture reading. Students in this phase need instruction in attending to all the letter-sound correspondences in words, segmenting each sound, and blending the sounds to read the word.

The writing of a child moving toward the partial-alphabetic phase of reading development

Similarly, when students in the partial-alphabetic phase attempt to spell a word, they often capture only some of the letter-sound correspondences in that word. That said, they may have a few words securely stored, or mapped, in memory, especially high-frequency words that have received a lot of attention in the classroom—*the, of, said*—but mostly their spellings reflect attempts to use their newly acquired letter-sound and phoneme segmentation skills. For example, in the sample at left, kindergartener Callie writes an important message: the kitchen.

The writing of a child in the partial-alphabetic phase of reading development

She is clearly in the partial-alphabetic phase, as demonstrated by her brilliant use of basic letter-sound knowledge that she applied to the most salient sounds in the word *kitchen*.

Over her kindergarten year, as her teacher moved through the phonics scope and sequence, and her knowledge of letter-sound correspondences increased, Callie became stronger at segmenting sounds in words she heard and spelling words. That enabled her to represent almost every sound needed to write the sentence: *I rode my scooter*. In fact, the only sound that is missing is the /r/ sound at the end of *scooter*! Her writing shows that she is well on her way into the full-alphabetic phase.

Benchmarks Related to Orthographic Mapping

Check for these behaviors and understandings to make sure your students are making steady gains.

KINDERGARTEN

- Segments and blends sounds in spoken one-syllable words (e.g., /t/ /r/ /u/ /ck/ into *truck*)
- Creates new words by changing the first phoneme in spoken one-syllable words (e.g., *mice* to *dice* to *rice*)
- Knows names of uppercase and lowercase letters
- Knows the most common sound of each letter
- Decodes basic consonant-vowel-consonant (CVC) words and other one-syllable words
- Represents some sounds in words when spelling them, using reasonable letter representations

GRADE 1

- Segments, blends, and manipulates the sounds in one-syllable words, including words with consonant blends (e.g., *st*, *fl*)
- Creates new words by changing the phonemes in spoken one-syllable words
- Knows the letter-sound correspondences for common blends and digraphs (e.g., *ph*, *th*)
- Decodes regularly spelled one-syllable words
- Decodes long-vowel sounds using the VC*e* rule (e.g., *cane*, *time*)
- Decodes two-syllable words that are compound words comprised of known words (e.g., *bathtub*) or that follow basic syllable patterns

The Tension Between Reading and Spelling in Grades K and 1

Let's revisit Katie's representation of children's reading and spelling development as two points on a rubber band. In kindergarten and first grade, reading and spelling skills are typically aligned so the rubber band is slack.

For some students, at the end of first grade, the first signs of reading skills progressing faster than spelling skills begin to appear. That is often due to the introduction of various ways to spell a sound, which often entail two letters. Digraphs, VC*e* words, and, later on, vowel teams and *r*-controlled vowels all add to the complexity of spelling. Reading is an easier skill because it involves recognition—the letters are given so students just need to match the sounds to them and blend them together. Spelling, on the other hand, requires students to reproduce the word by first segmenting each sound and then deciding how to represent the sound from all the letter-sound combinations they know.

Things typically start off well, or the rubber band is slack, when students are reproducing or spelling CVC words in kindergarten. However, not long after, tension may occur in the rubber band for students who can sound out and eventually automatically recognize a word when reading, but they struggle to reproduce the word accurately in their spelling.

Therefore, ensuring students have systematic spelling instruction, in addition to word reading instruction, is critical to supporting the progression of both skills.

The Instructional Routine for Grades K and 1

To make a word stick in memory, young children need to analyze it in multiple ways: say the word, segment its sounds, spell it, understand its meaning, and read it multiple times. Our four-step routine, which we explained in the previous chapter, ensures that kind of deep word analysis. Specifically, children (1) See & Say the word, (2) Segment & Spell the word, (3) Study & Suss Out the word, and (4) Search & Stick the word. These rich levels of analysis clarify and strengthen connections between the spelling, pronunciation, and meaning of the word—the key ingredients for orthographic mapping!

A Menu of Activities

The table below provides a menu of activities for each step of our routine for kindergarten to first grade. When teaching a new word, select four activities—one from each column—and carry them out in the order of the routine. We encourage you to try all the activities; just remember, choose just one per column and follow the routine to ensure students are engaged and analyzing words deeply. Consider how you might mix and match activities from the menu.

Watch Katie carry out the grades K–1 routine.

Choose one activity from each column and teach them in order.

 STEP 1 See & Say	 STEP 2 Segment & Spell	STEP 3 Study & Suss Out	STEP 4 Search & Stick
• See It, Call It • See It, Say It, Sing It/ Shout It/Robot It • See It, Say It, Mirror It • See It, Say It, Jump It	• Tap It, Spell It • Count It, Map It • Word Chain It • March It, Spell It • Tap It, Unscramble It	• Sketch It • Act It Out • Picture It • Check Its Use • Know Its Many Meanings • Word Parts **Function Words:** • Hear It, Use It • Choose It, Use It	• Sort It • Swat It • Hunt for It

Place Your Order

Let's use this menu of activities to see how one teacher "places an order" to support orthographic mapping in a first-grade classroom. For her first week of instruction, first-grade teacher Julie is covering CVC words with the short /i/ sound, such as *tin*, *pig*, *rip* (all consonant sounds have been taught). Julie decided to do the following routine:

Steps From the Routine	Activities Selected by Julie
See & Say	See It, Say It, Sing It
Segment & Spell	Tap It, Unscramble It
Study & Suss Out	Sketch It
Search & Stick	Swat It

Julie uses the routine in each of her word-work/phonics lessons that week, adding to the group of CVC words with the target letter-sound short /i/: *hit*, *bit*, *rim*, *kin*, *sip*, *dim*, *pit*, *fit*, *kit*, *yip*, *him*. Using the same routine for the entire week with first graders is wise because it maximizes her students' opportunity to master the CVC short /i/ pattern, while being exposed to many words, including vocabulary words *dim*, *kin*, and *yip*.

When Julie moves along her scope and sequence for the next week—to CVC words with the short /e/ sound, such as *set*, *met*, *pen*, *hen*—she changes the routine to keep her students' interest and engagement high.

Steps From the Routine	Activities Selected by Julie
See & Say	See It, Say It, Jump It
Segment & Spell	Count It, Map It
Study & Suss Out	Check Its Use
Search & Stick	Sort It

Download lesson planning sheets.

Julie uses this routine in each of her small-group lessons and centers all week, adding CVC words with the short /e/ sound: *peg*, *leg*, *men*, *get*, *bed*, *bet*, *hen*, *led*, *red*. Her students had ample opportunity to see, say, segment, spell, use, and read those words. The activities provide targeted, explicit, systematic, multimodal instruction to support mastery of the CVC short /e/ pattern and, ultimately, storage of words in long-term memory.

Activity Instructions and Scripts

On pages 58 to 76, we provide instructions and a short script for each activity in the routine. The purpose of the scripts is to clarify the steps for each activity as well as provide possible language to use with students. Feel free to modify our language, of course, to fit your own teaching style and goals and the needs of your students.

Download all the student activity pages in this chapter.

Throughout the scripts, we use the target word *bat* not only because it is a CVC word that students typically learn in K–1, but also because its multiple meanings provide an opportunity to teach vocabulary as well as phonics.

Our Recommended Phonics Scope and Sequence for Kindergarten and Grade 1

Use it to select words for the activities.

- Alphabet Knowledge
- Consonants and Short Vowels
- Consonant Blends
- Consonant Digraphs
- Less Complex Long Vowels (e.g., long vowels with a final *e*)

The Many Meanings of *Bat*

Here are the meanings of *bat* as a noun:

- A flying nocturnal animal with fangs
- What you use to hit a ball in sports such as baseball

As a verb, *bat* can mean:

- To hit or swat at something

We also show what happens to *bat* when we add inflected endings; for example:

batty: crazy, nutty, or wild

batting: the action of hitting or using a bat or the cotton stuffing used in a quilt

Step 1: See & Say

These are the menu options for See & Say, the step in the routine that helps students connect the written word to its phonological representation, or pronunciation. Our goal is for students to see the word, hear it spoken, and say it themselves.

See It, Call It

Materials

- Word written so students can see it
- Auditory feedback phones/reading phones

WHAT: Rosenthal and Ehri (2011) found that orally saying words enhanced vocabulary word learning more than reading words silently. Auditory feedback phones, also called reading phones, allow students to hear their voice amplified, which provides immediate phonological feedback. In this activity, students look at the word, say the word, and then use a reading phone to say the word again.

HOW: The script below serves to jumpstart your directions and conversation. The **T** is teacher-directed language, and the **S** indicates what students do.

T: Look at this word. It is *bat*. Say it.

S: *bat*

T: Pick up your reading phone and say the word while I point to it.

T: (Points to the word.)

S: (Students pick up phones.) *bat*

TIPS

- Make sure students wipe off the phones with an antibacterial wipe before storing them in a secure bag or box.
- Make the reading phones out of PVC piping or buy them from your local or online teacher store.

See It, Say It, Sing It/Shout It/Robot It

Materials

- Word written so students can see it

WHAT: Students look at the word, say it, and then sing or shout it, or say it in a robot voice. As Richard Gentry and Gene Ouellette (2025) remind us, the goal is to "bombard or flood students with sounds to tune up the hearing and sound-processing brain areas known to be involved in the neurological reading circuit."

HOW: The script below serves to jumpstart your directions and conversation. The **T** is teacher-directed language, and the **S** indicates what students do.

> T: Look at this word. It is *bat*. Say it.
>
> S: *bat*
>
> T: Now say it in your best singing voice (or shouting or robot voice), like this (sings/shouts/robots the word *bat*). You try.
>
> S: *bat* (in singing/shouting/robot voice)

TIPS

- Have fun using your singing voice! Take the word *bat* and go up and down on an octave scale or pretend it is the last note you are hitting in the opera.
- Robot voice is a great option when volume and silliness need to be kept in check.

STEP 1

See & Say

See It, Say It, Mirror It

Materials

- Word written so students can see it
- Pocket mirrors/handheld mirrors
- Articulation cards from your classroom sound wall (if available)

WHAT: Images of mouth formations, otherwise known as articulation cards, help students learn letter-sound correspondences (Loftus & Sappington, 2024). They provide visual reminders of what's happening in students' mouths when they say a sound and connect it to a letter. Pocket mirrors, a device long used by speech language pathologists to assist students in articulation, allow students to examine their tongue, lips, and teeth as they produce letter sounds.

HOW: The script below serves to jumpstart your directions and conversation. The **T** is teacher-directed language, and the **S** indicates what students do.

T: Look at this word. It is *bat*. Say it.

S: *bat*

T: Pick up your mirrors.

T: (Points to the first letter in the word.) See how my lips come together to make the /b/ sound? I bring my lips together before pushing it out to make that sound. Now you try it.

- If you've got articulation cards, point out the proper lip positioning.

S: (Students pick up mirrors and examine mouth formation in /b/ sound.)

- **T:** (Potential prompting questions) What do you see in the mirror? How do your lips look?

T: Let's use the mirrors to see how our mouths look for the /a/ sound. Watch me. To make this sound, I open my mouth halfway. I feel the tip of my tongue against the back of my bottom teeth. Now you try it.

- If you've got articulation cards, point out the proper lip positioning.

S: (Students pick up mirrors and examine mouth formation in /a/ sound.)

- **T:** (Potential prompting questions) What do you see in the mirror? How do your lips look?

T: (Points to the last letter in the word.) The last sound is the /t/ sound. I can't see it, but I feel how I move my tongue up to touch the bumps on the roof of my mouth to make this sound. Now you try it.

S: (Students pick up mirrors and examine mouth formation in /t/ sound.)

- **T:** (Potential prompting questions) What do you see in the mirror? How do your lips look?

T: Now let's look in the mirrors as we push all of these sounds together in the word *bat*. You try it.

S: (Students look in mirrors while saying, /b//a//t/, *bat*.)

TIPS

- Your school's speech language pathologist is your best ally in articulation and sound walls.
- The mouth positioning in short vowels changes minimally from sound to sound, so it's often more challenging for young children to notice these differences.
- Use articulation cards depicting diverse students, like the examples below, or create your own cards by photographing your students making the sounds.

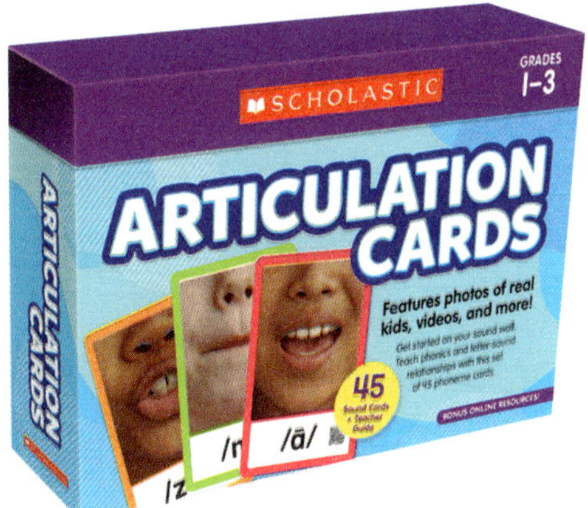

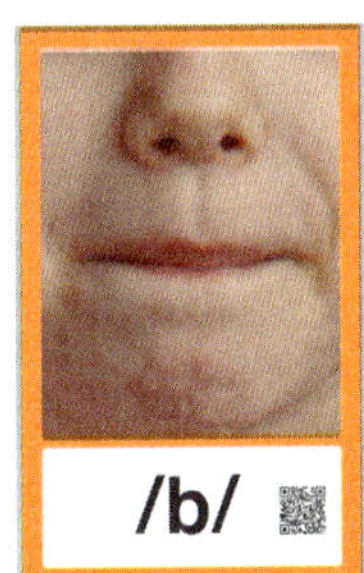

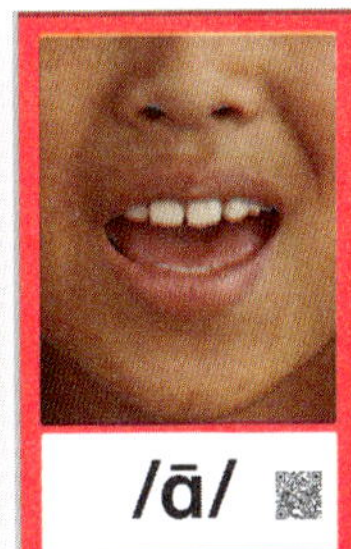

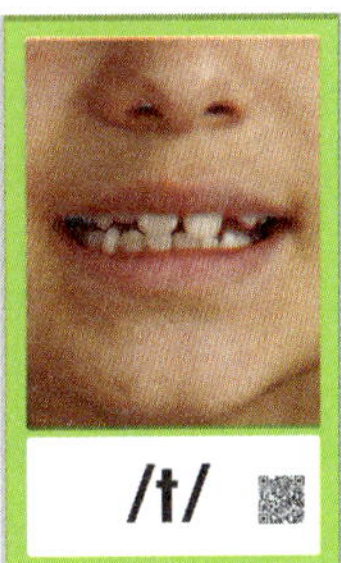

STEP 1

See & Say

See It, Say It, Jump It

Materials

- Word written so students can see it

WHAT: With this activity, students see and say the word, and jump for each syllable while they say it again, adding kinesthetic movement to the auditory representation of the word.

HOW: The script below serves to jumpstart your directions and conversation. The **T** is teacher-directed language, and the **S** indicates what students do.

T: Look at this word. It is *bat*. Say it.

S: *bat*

T: Remember that a syllable is is a whole word or part of a word that has one vowel sound. Now jump for each syllable you hear in *bat*.

S: *bat* (while jumping one time)

TIPS

- This activity can be used for single-syllable and multisyllabic words.
- If jumping is not possible for your students, or if it gets too out of hand for some students, have them squat, raise their arms in the air, etc., to get some movement into the activity.

Step 2: Segment & Spell

STEP 2

These are the menu options for Segment & Spell, the step in the routine in which students analyze the sounds of the word and match the appropriate letters to those sounds. As a result, they make grapheme (letter)-phoneme (sound) connections that help store the word in long-term memory.

Tap It, Spell It

Materials

- Word written so students can see it
- Dry-erase boards and markers

WHAT: Students say the word and then segment the sounds they hear in it by tapping a finger on the table, starting with their thumb. Then they attempt to spell each sound on a dry-erase board. A robust body of research indicates that instruction in phonology—analyzing grapheme-phoneme correspondences—produces positive student outcomes (Foorman et al., 2016).

HOW: The script below serves to jumpstart your directions and conversation. The **T** is teacher-directed language, and the **S** indicates what students do.

T: Look at this word. It is *bat*. Say it.

S: *bat*

T: Now segment each sound you hear in the word *bat* by tapping a finger on the table. Watch me. (Models: /b/a/t/.) Your turn.

S: /b/ /a/ /t/ (Students tap a finger on the table for each sound.)

T: Now spell each sound you hear in *bat*. Use your finger taps if you need help identifying the sound you need to spell.

S: (Students use a dry-erase board and marker to spell the word.)

T: Now let's check our work. (Shows board with the word spelled.)

S: (Students correct any errors.)

TIP

Teachers should model what to do when students get stuck with their spelling—tap again and stop at the sound that needs letter(s) representation.

Count It, Map It

Materials

- Word written so students can see it
- Count and Box Letters (Appendix B)
- Small color chips for counting or any kind of counter

WHAT: We've found that students enjoy this activity a lot, and teachers find it especially effective. Students segment the sounds in a word, move a chip into each box on the Count and Box Letters sheet, and then represent each sound in writing, as explored in a 2000 article by Laurice Joseph. This activity is a modification of Elkonin sound boxes, the instructional legacy of D. B. Elkonin (1973), who used them to link phonemic awareness to letters. In a 2019 literature review, Kelsey Ross and Laurice Joseph indicated the power of word boxes to help preschool through elementary students acquire phonemic awareness, letter-sound correspondence knowledge, and spelling skills.

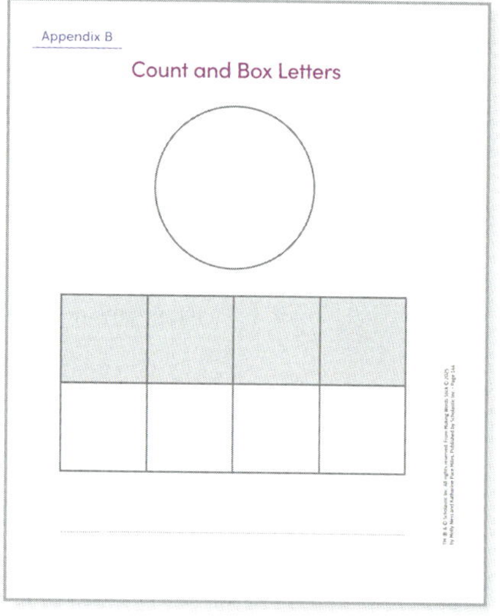

HOW: The script below serves to jumpstart your directions and conversation. The **T** is teacher-directed language, and the **S** indicates what students do.

T: Look at this word. It is *bat*. Say it.

S: *bat*

T: Now I'm going to cover the word. (Covers word.) Watch as I move a chip for each sound I say in the word into a sound box. (Models word.) Now you do it.

S: (Students move a chip as they say each sound, /b/ /a/ /t/.)

T: I will say each sound in *bat*, and you will check to see if you have the right number of chips. /b/ /a/ /t/.

S: (Students check to see if they have a chip in three boxes.)

> **TIP**
> You have several options for "chips." Consider using coins, small counters used for math, or figurines of any kind. Dot stampers also work well.

T: Now write the letter that represents each sound in the box below the chip.

S: (Students write the letter that represents each sound: /b/*b*, /a/*a*, /t/*t*.)

T: Now let's check our work. (Shows board with the word spelled.)

S: (Students correct any errors.)

Word Chain It

Materials

- Magnetic letters or letter tiles

WHAT: A word chain builds phonemic awareness, decoding (word reading), and encoding (spelling) skills by encouraging students to change one sound (phoneme) in a word to create a new word. Because students are changing just one sound, they must hold the word's other sounds in memory while they decide how to create the new word. Additionally, with each new word, students must decide the letter (grapheme) that represents the sound necessary to create that word. The 2016 Institute of Education Sciences (IES) report uses the terminology "word-building exercises" to show how word chains "enhance students' awareness of how words are composed and how each letter or phoneme in a word contributes to its spelling and pronunciation" (also see Rashotte et al., 2001).

HOW: The script below serves to jumpstart your directions and conversation. The **T** is teacher-directed language, and the **S** indicates what students do.

T: Today we are going to be building word chains. (Pulls out the letters for the chosen set of target words and places them on the table above the whiteboard.)

T: What sounds do you hear in the word *bat*?

S: (Students point a finger for each sound while saying, /b/ /a/ /t/.)

T: Now make the word *hat* using the letters. (Provides corrective feedback as needed.)

S: (Students make the word.)

T: Now read the word.

S: (Students read the word.)

T: Now how many sounds do you hear in the word *hat*?

S: (Students point a finger for each sound while saying, /h/ /a/ /t/.)

T: Now make the word *ham* by only taking away, adding, or changing the letters that need to be changed. (Provides corrective feedback as needed.)

S: (Students make the word.)

T: (If students select or take away the wrong letter, asks: "What sound does that letter make? What sound does this new word ____ need?")

T: (Prompts students to read each word when it is built by saying, "Read the word.")

S: (Students read the word.)

T: (Repeats cycle by forming a new word.)

TIP

Differentiate this activity by adding extra letters for students to choose from. Some students do not need any extra letters when they first do this activity—it is enough for them to distinguish between the group of target letters that will all be used to make the words in the chain. Other students may be ready to have a few extra letters to challenge their letter-sound and phonemic awareness discrimination skills.

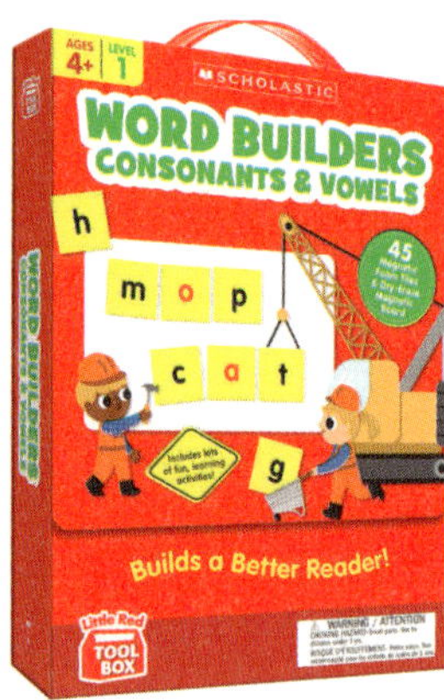

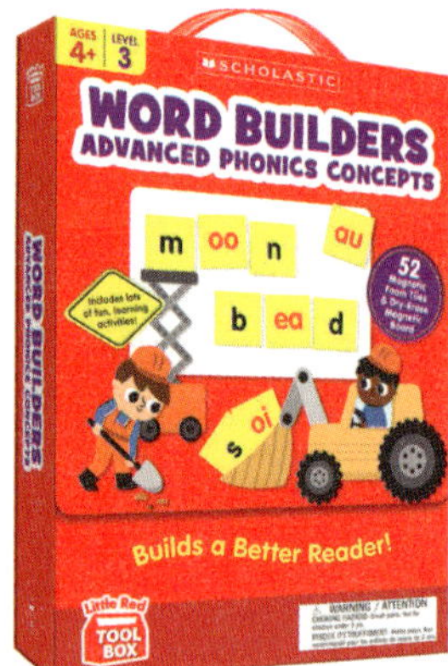

March It, Spell It

Materials

- Word written so students can see it
- Dry-erase board and marker or paper and pencil

WHAT: Let's get up and move! This kinesthetic activity is meant to increase engagement to accomplish a critical phonemic awareness task—segmenting individual sounds in words (Brady, 2020). Students segment the sounds in the word by marching in place. Then they spell the word.

HOW: The script below serves to jumpstart your directions and conversation. The **T** is teacher-directed language, and the **S** indicates what students do.

T: Look at this word. It is *bat*. Say it.

S: *bat*

T: Now let's stand up and march for each sound we hear in the word. Watch me: /b/ (march), /a/ (march), /t/ (march). Your turn.

S: /b/ (march), /a/ (march), /t/ (march).

T: Now spell the word on your board, and quietly march under the table if needed.

S: (Students spell the word, and quietly march if needed.)

T: Now let's check our work. (Shows board with the word spelled.)

S: (Students correct any errors.)

TIP

If standing and marching is not possible, stomping feet while remaining seated, or tapping feet on the floor while seated are reasonable alternatives to keep some movement in the activity.

STEP 2

Segment & Spell

Tap It, Unscramble It

Materials

- Word written so students can see it
- Letter tiles or magnetic letters

WHAT: This activity ensures students have fun encoding, or spelling, the word by putting mixed-up letter tiles or magnetic letters in the correct order. Paige Pullen and Holly Lane note the effectiveness of manipulatives—such as letter tiles and magnetic letters—in building early literacy skills (2016).

HOW: The script below serves to jumpstart your directions and conversation. The **T** is teacher-directed language, and the **S** indicates what students do.

T: Look at this word. It is *bat*. Say it.

S: *bat*

T: Watch as I count (or tap) the sounds in *bat*. (Holds up a finger for each sound in the word: /b/ /a/ /t/.) Now you try.

S: (Students hold up a finger for each sound: /b/ /a/ /t/.)

T: Now watch as I unscramble this set of magnetic letters to spell *bat*. (Slides the *b*, *a*, *t* out of the pile of six letters to spell the word.) Now you try to unscramble the letters.

S: (Students select the letters and slide them to spell *bat*.) (First time)

T: Now scramble the letters back up and spell *bat* again. (Models gently scrambling the letters again.)

S: (Students scramble their pile of letters and then spell *bat* again.) (Second time)

T: Now scramble the letters and spell *bat* one last time.

S: (Students scramble the letters and then spell *bat* again.) (Third time)

TIPS

- **Magnetic letters or letter tiles work well, or you can use cut-up squares of paper with the letters written on them (a paper version of letter tiles).**
- **Allow older students to use digital tile boards available on free apps or websites to eliminate the stigma of the magnetic letters or tiles being for younger students.**

Step 3: Study & Suss Out

These are the menu options for Study & Suss Out, the step in the routine in which students activate the meaning of the word. Our goal is for them to understand the definition, possible multiple meanings, and correct usage of the word.

Sketch It

Materials

- Word written so students can see it
- Simple art supplies (e.g., chart paper, drawing paper, markers, crayons)

WHAT: Visual representations strengthen and clarify understanding of word meanings—and help students retain those meanings, particularly for multilingual learners and/or neurodivergent students. This activity gets you and your students creating those representations, a recommendation made by James Baumann and colleagues (2003).

HOW: The script below serves to jumpstart your directions and conversation. The **T** is teacher-directed language, and the **S** indicates what students do.

T: The word is *bat*. Watch as I quickly draw a picture of the animal that flies in the night sky. (Sketches a bat.) I've made sure to include wings and fangs, because those are two important characteristics of bats. Now it's your turn to draw a bat. You can make it look like mine, or you can add other details if you'd like. You have one minute. (Sets a timer.)

S: (Students sketch a bat.)

T: Remind me what *bat* means?

S: (Students provide the definition.)

T. There is another kind of bat. It's the long stick-like object that a baseball player holds to hit the ball. Watch as I draw that kind of bat. (Sketches a baseball bat.) I've included a ball next to my bat to remind me that I'm using the bat that goes along with the sport of baseball. Now it's your turn to draw this type of bat.

TIPS

- Avoid a mini art lesson! A simple pencil sketch is fine.
- To keep this activity succinct, use a projected timer to count down the remaining time.
- It's natural for us to dismiss our artistic skills with statements like, "I'm a terrible artist". Try to resist that urge!

You can make it look like mine, or you can add other details if you'd like. You have one minute. (Sets a timer.)

S: (Students sketch a baseball bat.)

T: Remind me what this *bat* means?

S: (Students provide the definition.)

Act It Out

Materials

- Word written so students can see it

WHAT: Remember Charades? The aim here is to reinforce word meanings by having students act them out, using facial expressions and body movements, rather than words. Nonverbal supports, like gestures, miming, and hand or body movements have been found to increase student vocabulary and language outcomes (Barnes et al., 2023).

HOW: The script below serves to jumpstart your directions and conversation. The **T** is teacher-directed language, and the **S** indicates what students do.

T: The word is *bat*. I'm going to use a body movement to show what the word means. If I were a baseball player holding a bat, I'd hold that bat in my hands like this (demonstrates holding a bat). I'd swing the bat like this (demonstrates swinging a bat) to try to hit the ball. Now show me how you swing a bat.

S: (Students demonstrate swinging a bat.)

T: Well done. Remind me what *bat* means.

S: (Students provide meaning of the word.)

TIPS

- It is often easier to act out nouns or verbs, so consider what words you are using.
- If you're struggling to come up with how to act out or use body movement for a particular word, students may struggle as well. Another activity may be better suited for that word.

Picture It

Materials

- Word written so students can see it
- Images of your target word, including clip art, digital images, illustrations, photographs, etc.

WHAT:

Students are more likely to grasp a word's meaning(s) when they hear the word, see the word, and see an image representing the word (Perfetti, 2007). Lean into the power of images by showing them as you discuss word meanings with students.

HOW: The script below serves to jumpstart your directions and conversation. The **T** is teacher-directed language, and the **S** indicates what students do.

T: The word is *bat*. I'm going to show you what a bat looks like. (Shows a digital image of a bat from a simple internet search). When I look at this picture, I see that the bat has wings and fangs. What else do you notice about this picture?

S: (Students comment on what they observe about the picture.)

T: Let's look at another image of the same word. What do you see here? (Shows a picture of a baseball bat.)

S: (Students comment on what they observe about the picture.)

T: So what are the two definitions of *bat*?

S: (Students respond without the pictures.)

TIP

When possible, bringing in a physical object improves students' understanding of the word. For instance, when working with the word *shell*, you might pass around a seashell for students to touch and hold, as well as the pasta shape that are also called *shells*!

STEP 3

Study & Suss Out

Check Its Use

Materials

- Word written so students can see it

WHAT: In addition to knowing a word's meanings, students must understand when it is used appropriately or inappropriately. We encourage students to apply words through oral wordplay, where they identify if a word is being used correctly, or not. We've modified this activity from Isabel Beck and her colleagues (2013).

HOW: The script below serves to jumpstart your directions and conversation. The **T** is teacher-directed language, and the **S** indicates what students do.

T: Let's play some riddles with our target word *bat*. I'm going to give you some clues. If the clues match our target word *bat*, say the word aloud. If the clues don't match, don't say anything at all.

- An animal that walks on the ground (S: Students don't say anything.)
- An animal that flies at night (S: *bat*)
- Something you use to hit a ball (S: *bat*)
- Something that you throw with (S: Students don't say anything.)

S: (Students correctly respond to prompts. See above.)

T: Remind me what the word *bat* means?

TIPS

- Brainstorm clues in advance. It's hard to think of them on the spot!
- Spice up the ways in which your students respond: Clapping, shouting, or stomping for the correct use of the word are just a few possibilities.

Know Its Many Meanings

Materials

- Word written so students can see it

WHAT: Being able to use a word appropriately in a sentence is the ultimate goal of vocabulary learning! Here, students are given a word with multiple meanings; they write sentences that demonstrate their understanding of each meaning, an instructional recommendation provided in an article examining the complexities of vocabulary application of multiple-meaning words (Booton et al., 2022).

HOW: The script below serves to jumpstart your directions and conversation. The **T** is teacher-directed language, and the **S** indicates what students do.

> **T:** The word is *bat*. Turn to your partner. The person sitting closest to the door will come up with a sentence for the *bat* that flies, and the other partner will come up with a sentence for the *bat* that hits. Take a minute to think of a juicy sentence with details. Okay, Partner 1, closest to the door, share your sentence.
>
> **S:** (Partner 1 shares a sentence referring to the animal.)
>
> **T:** Okay, now Partner 2, take a minute to think of a sentence with juicy details. Okay, Partner 2, share your sentence.
>
> **S:** (Partner 2 shares a sentence referring to the sports equipment.)
>
> **T:** Who would like to nominate their partner to share their sentence because it had so many juicy details?

TIP

We've seen teachers come up with clever ways to pair up students by, for example, giving them stickers of cookies and milk (or any other common pairings—burgers and fries, beans and rice, Bert and Ernie) on the floor. The teacher simply says, "Cookies, you create a sentence for the first definition of *bat*, and Milk, you create a sentence for the other definition of *bat*."

STEP 3

Study & Suss Out

Word Parts

Materials

- Word written so students can see it
- Word Part Organizer on a piece of chart paper (Appendix C)

WHAT: Students determine the meaning of a word by identifying the meanings of its parts. Here we are building students' early word-analysis skills, or their ability to study morphemes as units of meaning (Bowers et al., 2010).

HOW: The script below serves to jumpstart your directions and conversation. The **T** is teacher-directed language, and the **S** indicates what students do.

Morpheme Example

T: We have been working with the word *bat*. Now I'm going to change the word to *batty* and *batting*. Say these words as I point to them.

S: *batty*, *batting*

T: The first definition of *bat* we learned was a flying animal with fangs that comes out at night. Let's underline the word *bat* in *batty* and write *bat* in the first box. (Underlines *bat* and writes it in the first box on the chart paper.)

T: When the -*y* is added to the end of the word, it changes *bat* into an adjective that describes a person, place, or thing. I'm going to double the *t* in *bat* and put the -*y* into the second box. The -*y* attached to *bat* means someone who is acting like a flying bat. Now this doesn't mean they are biting people. Instead, it means someone who is acting wild. When bats fly around they are a bit wild; they swoop all over the place. So if someone is described as *batty*, they are being crazy or wild.

T: Stand up and act batty.

S: (Students act out *batty*.)

T: Now let's look at the two parts of *batty* again and say it together.

S: *batty*

T: Okay, the next word is *batting*. Watch as I underline *bat*. (Underlines *bat* and writes it in the first box on the chart paper.) I'm going to double the *t* in *bat* and put the *-ing* into the second box. When *-ing* is added to the word *bat* it means using the bat to hit the ball or hitting something so it goes away. The *-ing* turns the word into a verb, or action word.

T: Stand up and act out *batting*.

S: (Students act out *batting*.)

T: Now let's look at the two parts of *batting* again and say it together.

S: *batting*

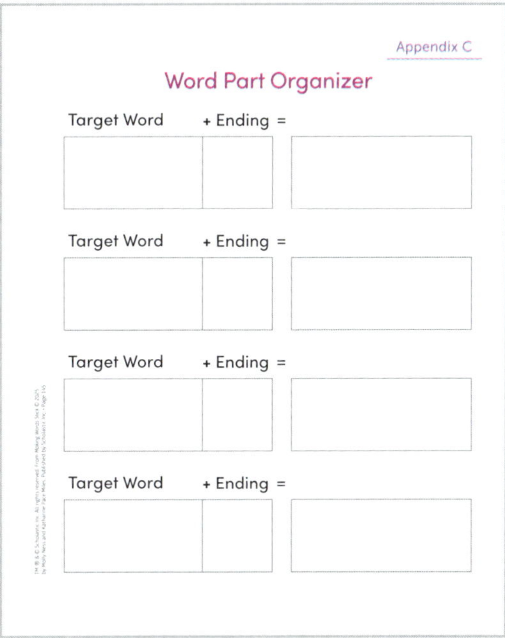
Appendix C

Word Part Organizer

Target Word	+ Ending =	

Target Word	+ Ending =	

Target Word	+ Ending =	

Target Word	+ Ending =	

Compound Word Example

T: In the word *baseball* there are two small words—*base* and *ball*. Let's use this Word Part Organizer to figure out the meaning of the word. (Draw the Word Part Organizer onto the chart paper.) What is the first small word you see in *baseball*?

S: *base*

T: I'm going to write *base* in the first box. Bases are small white square pads that are placed in a diamond shape to play this game. (Shows or draws a picture.)

T: What is the second small word you see in *baseball*?

S: *ball*

T: I'm going to write *ball* in the second box. A particular type of ball is used in this game. It is white with red stitching. (Shows or draws a picture.)

T: Now turn to your neighbor. Partner 2 defines the word *baseball* using what we know about what the small words mean.

S: (Partner 1 provides a definition to Partner 2. Partner 2 defines the next word.)

TIP

This activity can be used with any compound word or any word with more than one morpheme. Remember, simple endings of -*s*, -*y*, -*ly*, and -*ed* add meaning to a word.

Study & Suss Out: Function Words

There are many words that can't be defined or depicted—you need to use them to understand their meanings (Miles & Ehri, 2017; Miles et al., 2018). Function words such as *there*, *were*, and *its* are among them. Because function words are tricky to define, they need a specific type of activity for Study & Suss Out. In other words, use Steps 1, 2, and 4 for function words but the following substitutions for Step 3.

Hear It, Use It

Materials

- Word written so students can see it
- A set of word cards in small plastic bags that form a sentence and a question for each student (see guidelines below)

WHAT: Remember that function words have little meaning, but they signal grammatical relationships, hold semantic importance, and are the connective tissue of sentences (Miles et al., 2018). In this activity, students listen for the word in a sentence read to them, and then they create their own sentences containing the word (Ehri & Wilce, 1985). Thus, the activity provides exposure to the function words, in addition to application.

HOW: The script below serves to jumpstart your directions and conversation. The **T** is teacher-directed language, and the **S** indicates what students do.

Watch Molly carry out the routine for a function word.

T: Look at this word. It is *to*. Say it.

S: *to*.

T: Now listen to how the word *to* is used in this sentence, "I like to read books."

T: In this baggie, you have words that create a sentence. Please put them in order to create a sentence. There may be some words that you don't use. Just put those over to the side.

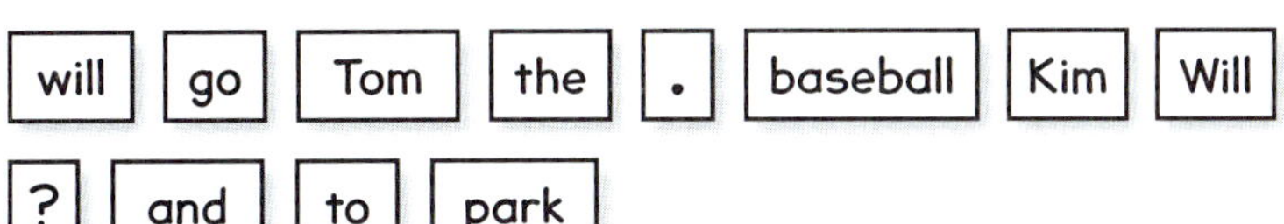

S: (Students empty their baggies and arrange the words in a sentence, including the punctuation card with a period on it.)

T: Read your sentence to a neighbor.

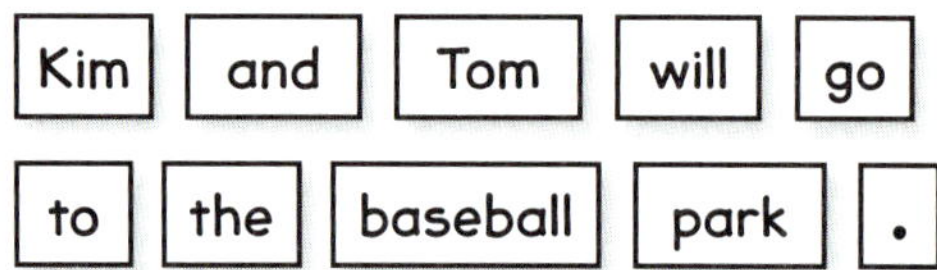

S: (Students read their sentence and make any corrections.)

T: Now find the punctuation card with a question mark on it. Create a question using the words. You may have different words that are left out this time.

S: (Students rearrange the words to create a question, including the punctuation card with a question mark on it.)

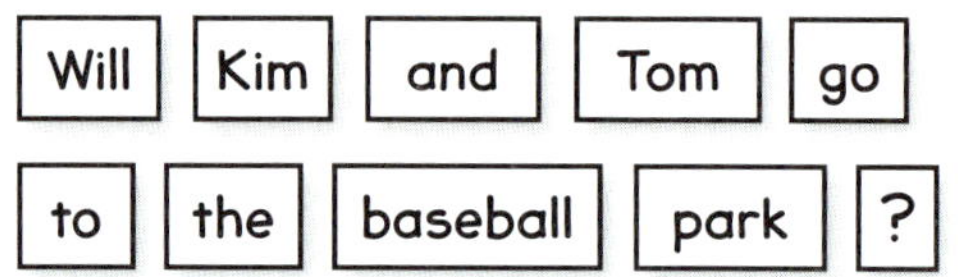

T: Read your question to a neighbor.

TIP

Students can make longer or shorter sentences depending on their sentence-generation abilities.

Choose It, Use It

Materials

- A paragraph with function words omitted or redacted

WHAT: In a 2018 article, Katie, Karen McFadden, and Linnea Ehri wrote that function words "rely on surrounding words for their meaning" and that they are particularly difficult to learn in isolation—when no information is available about the meaning or usage of the word. Logically, our function word instruction should focus more on usage and application. For this activity, students read a text with function words redacted. From there, they must think about possible words and incorporate them in a way that makes sense in the text.

HOW: The script below serves to jumpstart your directions and conversation. The **T** is teacher-directed language, and the **S** indicates what students do.

T: We are going to complete a paragraph that is missing some words! Read this to yourself and circle the word that makes the most sense when you come to the blank. Watch and listen as I do the first one. (Does the first line.) Now you try.

S: (Students begin reading the paragraph silently and circling the appropriate missing word.)

T: Now whisper-read your paragraph and see if you need to make any adjustments.

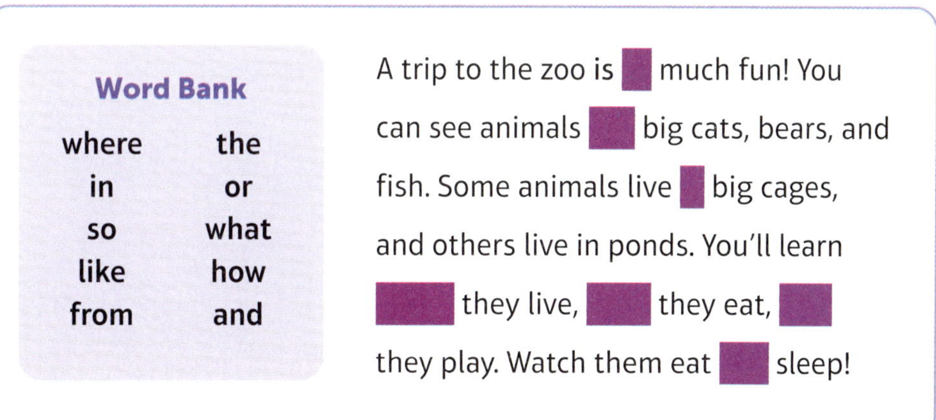

S: (Students whisper-read their paragraphs.)

T: Now read your paragraph to a partner. Take turns and make any corrections.

S: (Students take turns reading their paragraphs to their partners.)

T: Now let's read our paragraphs together and make any adjustments.

TIPS

- Provide students with a bank of function words to focus their attention on the best option for the paragraph's semantic structures.
- This is loosely related to the beloved game of Mad Libs, so students might appreciate making a connection between this activity and that game. But instead of being silly, as students typically would be when playing Mad Libs, they should focus on accurate usage/application of words.

Step 4: Search & Stick

STEP 4

These are the menu options for Search & Stick, the final step in the routine designed to help students automatically recognize the word. Our aim is immediate retrieval, efficiency, and connection to the word's use in text.

Sort It

Materials

- Small plastic bags
- Sets of 5–10 words with the new spelling pattern (e.g., *-at*) and 5–10 review words with a different spelling pattern (e.g., *-it*)

WHAT: Steacy and colleagues (2020) found that the characteristics of the word and the student's skills impacted the number of exposures needed to learn a new word. To increase the number of exposures to the target word and similarly spelled words, students should read the target word multiple times. For this activity, students quickly sort words into two categories: words with the new spelling pattern (*-at*) and a review spelling pattern (*-it*).

HOW: The script below serves to jumpstart your directions and conversation. The **T** is teacher-directed language, and the **S** indicates what students do.

T: We have been working on the word *bat*. Now sort this baggie of words into two columns: words that end in *-at* and words that we learned last week that end in *-it*.

S: (Students dump the baggie onto the table, find the colorful heading strips, and sort the words into the two piles.)

T: Now quietly read down both columns.

S: (Students quietly read the words in the columns.)

T: Now read these words to your partner. Partner 1 reads column 1, and Partner 2 reads column 2. Then switch columns.

S: (Students take turns reading aloud down each column.)

TIP

Consider using the word sort as a morpheme reinforcer. One column could have all the variations of the word (e.g., *bat*, *bats*, *batty*, *batting*, *batted*, *batter*). The other column could have the other target features (e.g., *-it* words) or a different word from the *-it* family with morphemic variations.

Swat It

Materials

- Fly swatter
- Five small squares of paper with a target word, 5–10 small squares with other words with a similar spelling pattern written on it

WHAT: To increase the number of exposures to the target word and similarly spelled words, provide students with opportunities to read the target word multiple times. One of the best, most entertaining ways to do that is to have students identify, read, and swat the word using a fly swatter! Just as we want to smack a fly with accuracy and speed, so too do we want students to recognize words!

HOW: The script below serves to jumpstart your directions and conversation. The **T** is teacher-directed language, and the **S** indicates what students do.

T: We have been working on the word *bat*. Now it's time to see how quickly you can find *bat* and other similar words with your swatter. Get ready!

S: (Students lift up their swatters.)

T: When I call out a word, you read the cards as you swat them. First, find all the *bat* cards.

S: (Students swat and read aloud all five *bat* cards.)

T: Now swat and read *hat*.

S: (Students swat and read *hat*.)

T: Now swat and read *cat*.

S: (Students swat and read *cat*.)

TIP

Students love this activity! You can cover a small table with word cards with the target word (*bat*) and the similarly spelled words. Then have students take turns, or have them play in pairs or small groups. You can also give each student a baggie of cards to swat at their desk as you call out the words.

Hunt for It

Materials

- Text
- Small sticky notes
- Decodable texts
- Magnifying glass (optional—just for fun!)

WHAT: It's not enough for students to recognize words in isolation; we must help them transfer—or extend what they've learned in word study instruction to connected text (Bransford et al., 1999).

HOW: The script below serves to jumpstart your directions and conversation. The **T** is teacher-directed language, and the **S** indicates what students do.

> **T:** We have been working with the word *bat*. Now we are going to read a book with the word *bat*. When you read the word *bat*, place one of these small sticky notes underneath it.
>
> **S:** (Students begin reading the book, and at the end of reading a sentence, they go back to underline the word *bat* with the sticky note.)
>
> **T:** Nice job reading the book. Now flip through the book and remove all the sticky notes while you read each underlined word.
>
> **S:** (Students read all the *bat* words as they remove the sticky notes.)

TIP

You may want to have more skilled students locate not only the target word, but also words that are phonetically similar. For instance, some students might be ready to hunt for CVC words with a short /a/ sound like in *bat*. This offers a differentiation opportunity for readers with more advanced phonetic skills.

In Closing, Remember...

As our pre-alphabetic and partial-alphabetic readers build their letter-sound correspondence knowledge and their phonemic-awareness skills, they begin their ascent into word reading and spelling! The initial incline is rocky, but enduring this rockiness is critical to eventually reach cruising altitudes. The Making Words Stick Menu for grades K and 1 cements those early reading skills that are the launchpad for orthographic mapping in the full-alphabetic phase.

Making Words Stick in Grades 2 and 3

CHAPTER 5

Imagine you are past the nail-biting initial ascent on an airplane, when things are bumpy, just as they are when you listen to a new reader decoding words. By this stage, students are in the last phase of their ascent, and by grade 3, students should have reached a smoother cruising altitude. Many words have already been stored in memory, and students' phonics skills are advancing, which results in less effort compared to grades K–1 reading and spelling.

Full-Alphabetic Readers

The vast majority of second and third graders are firmly in the full-alphabetic phase, and they are making strides toward the consolidated phase of word reading and spelling. By the end of second grade, based on the grade-level phonics scope and sequence, students should have learned a substantial number of phonetic concepts—all 44 phonemes, digraphs, and blends; "the bossy *e*"/VC*e* rule; all common vowel teams and most more advanced vowel teams; *r*-controlled vowels; common endings (e.g., *-le*, *-ing*, *-ed*); and common prefixes and suffixes. By the end of third grade, students move on to spelling rules (e.g., doubling consonants rule, dropping the *e* rule), more extensive prefix/suffix concepts (*pre-*, *bio-*, *-tion*, *-able*, *-ous*), and less common spelling patterns (e.g., *-eigh* says /a/, *-igh* says /i/, *-ere* says /air/). Because most students have attained all that phonetic and morphological knowledge, they're in a good position to unlock a wide body of words to read and spell accurately, and to understand the meaning of those words! By the end of third grade, students ideally transition into the consolidated alphabetic phase, in which students are reading and spelling multisyllabic words accurately on a routine basis.

The Tension Between Reading and Spelling in Grades 2 and 3

Remember the rubber band analogy that we introduced in Chapter 1? It serves as a reminder that reading and spelling don't always develop at the same rate because reading is based on recognizing letter-sound correspondences, which is easier than spelling or accurately reproducing letter-sound correspondences in order.

In second grade and above, you may see discrepancies between students' reading and spelling abilities because students are now spelling words that contain numerous letter combinations (/a/ = *a*, *a_e*, *ai*, *ay*, *ea*, *ei*, *eigh*, *ey*). If particular students struggle with spelling, you may wonder whether to move them forward in word reading or pause until their spelling catches up. Typically, the "reading" part of the rubber band leads, and the "spelling" part lags a bit behind, creating some tension. The tension should be manageable and simply require more opportunities to practice selecting the accurate phonetic element to represent the sound in a word.

If the rubber band becomes so taut that it may snap, students are likely applying their phonics knowledge to reading, but they have a weak orthographic representation of the word in memory. When this occurs, it's important to diagnose where students' spelling breakdowns occur to provide targeted, explicit support and lots of spelling practice. Often, students need additional opportunities to see how the word looks and hear how it sounds to access its spelling (Wasowicz, 2021).

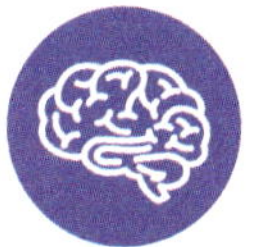

Benchmarks Related to Orthographic Mapping

Check for these behaviors and understandings to make sure your students are making steady gains.

GRADE 2

- Segments, blends, and manipulates the sounds in words (some readers may still need practice segmenting sounds in multisyllabic words for spelling)
- Applies phonics concepts from grade-level scope and sequence to read words accurately and spell words either accurately or with reasonable letter-sound patterns
- Decodes two-syllable words with regularly spelled phonic patterns and common prefixes and suffixes
- Has a corpus of high-frequency words (regularly or irregularly spelled) stored as sight words

GRADE 3

- Segments, blends, and manipulates the sounds in words (striving readers who are well behind grade level may need additional practice)
- Applies advanced phonics concepts, based on grade-level phonic scope and sequence, to read words accurately; spells most grade-level words (decodable and irregular) accurately; and spells words beyond grade level using letter-sound approximations (*anchor* spelled *anckor*)
- Decodes multisyllabic words by identifying prefixes, suffixes, roots, or any word part to determine pronunciation and meaning of the word
- Has a corpus of grade-level high-frequency words (regularly or irregularly spelled) stored as sight words

The Instructional Routine for Grades 2 and 3

To make words stick in memory in second and third grades, students need the same rigorous routine of saying the word, segmenting its sounds, spelling it, understanding its meaning, and reading the word multiple times. This kind of rich word analysis clarifies and strengthens connections between the spelling, pronunciation, and meaning of the word—the essential ingredients for orthographic mapping!

A Menu of Activities

The table below provides a menu of activities for each step of our routine. Just as we suggested for grades K–1, when teaching a new word, select four activities—one from each column—and carry them out in the order of the routine. We encourage you to try all the activities; just remember, choose just one per column and follow the routine to ensure students are engaged and analyzing words deeply. Consider how you might mix and match activities from the menu.

Watch Katie carry out the grades 2–3 routine.

Choose one activity from each column and teach them in order.

 STEP 1 See & Say	 STEP 2 Segment & Spell	STEP 3 Study & Suss Out	STEP 4 Search & Stick
• See It, Say It, Slide It • See It, Say It, Clap It • See It, Say It, Chin It • See It In Different Ways, Say It	• Count It, Box It, Spell It • Count It, Spell It Three Ways • Count It, Line It, Spell It	• Word Web It • Word Expert Card It • Paint Swatch It • Word Parts • Know Its Many Meanings • Word Ladder It **Function Words:** • Hear It, Use It • Choose It, Use It	• Hunt for It • Word Sorts • Find Its Look-Alike

Place Your Order

Let's use this menu of activities to see how one teacher "places an order" for orthographic mapping in a second-grade classroom. Second-grade teacher Douglas has covered common long vowel teams and *r*-controlled vowels, and is moving on to ambiguous vowel patterns. When teaching the pattern for the /aw/ sound spelled *aw* (such as *paw*, *saw*, *draw*), Douglas used the following sequence:

Steps From the Routine	Activities Selected by Douglas
See & Say	See It, Say It, Slide It
Segment & Spell	Count It, Line It, Spell It
Study & Suss Out	Paint Swatch It
Search & Stick	Find Its Look-Alike

He used the routine in each of his word work/phonics lessons that week, adding *claw, hawk, lawn, shawl*, and *straw*. When Douglas provides explicit instruction on the /aw/ sound spelled *au* the following week (e.g., *author*, *auction*, *caution*), he changes the routine to keep his students' interest and engagement high.

Steps From the Routine	Activities Selected by Douglas
See & Say	See It, Say It, Chin It
Segment & Spell	Count It, Spell It Three Ways
Study & Suss Out	Know Its Many Meanings
Search & Stick	Hunt for It

Download lesson planning sheets.

Douglas uses this routine for each of his small-group lessons and centers all week, adding *aw* and *au* words, eventually having his students compare and contrast the words that contain those two spelling patterns. With ample opportunity to see, say, segment sounds, spell, use, and read those words, students store them in long-term memory.

Activity Instructions and Scripts

On pages 91 to 115, we provide instructions and a short script for each activity and routine. The purpose of the scripts is to clarify the steps for each activity, as well as provide possible language to use with students. Feel free to modify our language, of course, to fit your own teaching style and goals and the needs of your students. Throughout the scripts, we use the target word *bridge,* not only because it has a more advanced spelling pattern of *-dge*, which students typically learn in second or third grade, but also because its multiple meanings provide an opportunity to teach vocabulary, as well as phonics.

Download all the student activity pages in this chapter.

Our Recommended Phonics Scope and Sequence for Grades 2 and 3

Use it to select words for the activities.

Long Vowel Teams

- Long *a* (*ai, ay*)
- Long *e* (*ee, ea*)
- Long *i* (*ie, igh*)
- Long *o* (*oa, ow*)
- Long *u* (*ew, ue*)
- Long *e* (*y, ey*)
- Long *i* (*y*)

Complex Vowels

- *r*-controlled vowels (*ar, or, ore, er, ir, ur*)
- Dipthongs (*oi, ou, ou, ow*)
- Variant vowels (*ai, au, aw*)

Inflectional Endings With Spelling Changes
(*y* to *i*, drop final *e*)

The Many Meanings of *Bridge*

Here are some meanings of *bridge* as a noun:

- A structure extending a road across a river, highway, railroad, or other obstacle
- The upper part of the nose, between the eyes
- An apparatus dentists use to replace missing teeth
- A card game that people play in groups of four
- A section of a piece of music that connects one part to another

We will also show what happens to *bridge* when inflected endings are added to it; for example:

Bridging

- The action of connecting two things
- To make the difference between two things smaller, as in "bridging the gap"

Step 1: See & Say

STEP 1

These are the menu options for See & Say, the step in the routine that helps students connect the written format of the word to its pronunciation. Our goal is for students to see the word, hear it spoken, and say it themselves.

See It, Say It, Slide It

Materials

- Word written so students can see it
- Word Blending (Appendix D)

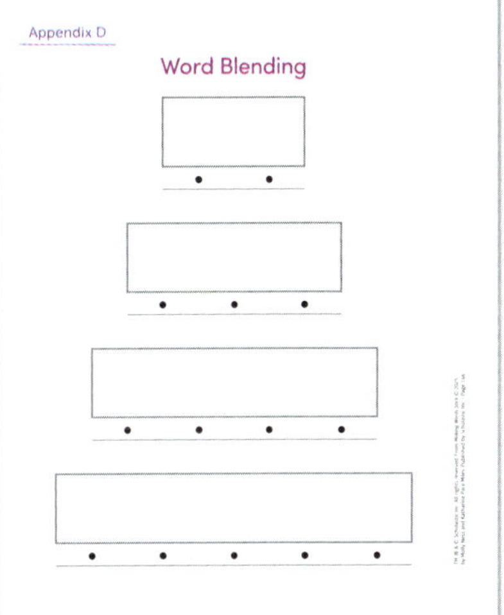

WHAT: The aim here is to build students' ability to blend a word's phonemes—that is, to sound out words without stopping between sounds (Gonzalez-Frey & Ehri, 2021). In this activity, students tap a finger for each sound in a word and then slide their finger across a line as they say the word.

HOW: The script below serves to jumpstart your directions and conversation. The **T** is teacher-directed language, and the **S** indicates what students do.

> **T:** Look at this word. It is *bridge*. Say it.
>
> **S:** *bridge*
>
> **T:** The sounds in *bridge* are /b//r//i//j/. Tap the dots on the long line for each sound, and then slide your finger across the line as you say *bridge*. Be sure to stop at the fourth dot. Now you try.
>
> **S:** (Students tap their fingers on each dot on the line as they say /b//r//i//j/. Then they start back at the beginning of the line and slide their fingers across the line, stopping at the fourth dot, while they say *bridge*.)

TIPS

- The lines on the Word Blending sheet contain multiple dots, allowing you to use it for words with two to five sounds. Each dot represents a sound. Tap a dot per sound, and then slide up to that dot when blending.
- To encourage continuous blending, provide students, especially younger students, with toy cars for "Drive It," and model how to drive the car smoothly between each letter.

STEP 1

See & Say

See It, Say It, Clap It

Materials

- Word written so students can see it

WHAT: Syllable awareness is a phonological sensitivity skill that prepares students to identify and study smaller units of sound. This is the classic approach to building that awareness by counting syllables in words, as recommended by the What Works Clearinghouse (Kamil et al., 2008).

HOW: The script below serves to jumpstart your directions and conversation. The **T** is teacher-directed language, and the **S** indicates what students do.

T: Look at this word. It is *bridge*. Say it.

S: *bridge*

T: Watch as I clap the word parts or syllables in *bridge*. (Claps one time—*bridge*.) Your turn.

S: (Claps one time and says *bridge*.)

T: Now look at this word. It is *bridging*. Say it.

S: *bridging*

T: Watch as I clap the word parts or syllables in *bridging*. (Claps twice—*bridging*.) Your turn.

S: (Students clap two times and say *bridging*.)

T: Remind me how many syllables *bridge* has. How many times did you clap? (Pause for responses) Remind me how many syllables *bridging* has. How many times did you clap?

TIP

Be on the lookout for students who are trying to blend in with the group by clapping when others are clapping. Are they clapping after everyone else? If so, they may need additional support.

See It, Say It, Chin It

Materials

- Word written so students can see it

WHAT: Phonological awareness, which includes syllable awareness, is a critical precursor to developing literacy skills (Phillips et al., 2008). This multisensory activity helps students identify and count syllables in words, as recommended in the IES guides. Connecting the mouth to immediate tactile feedback may help some students better identify syllables (Moats & Farrell, 2005).

HOW: The script below serves to jumpstart your directions and conversation. The **T** is teacher-directed language, and the **S** indicates what students do.

T: Look at this word. It is *bridge*. Say it.

S: *bridge*

T: Place your hand under your chin and say the word. Count the number of times your chin drops. Watch me. (Places flat hand horizontally under chin and says *bridge*.) Your turn.

S: (Students place hands under chins and say the word *bridge*.)

T: How many times did your hand drop?

S: Once!

T: Now let's try this with the word *bridging*. Watch the hand on my chin as I say *bridging*. (Places flat hand horizontally under chin and says *bridging*.) Your turn.

S: (Students place hands under chins and say the word *bridging*.)

T: How many times did your hand drop?

S: Twice!

TIPS

- Sometimes students (and teachers) exaggerate the pronunciations of words while doing this activity, which can distract from counting the word's syllables. Just say the word as you typically would in conversation.
- If the hand drop feels too subtle, mirrors may be useful.

STEP 1

See & Say

See It Different Ways, Say It

Materials

- Word written in a variety of fonts and/or in cursive so students can see it

WHAT: When students read, they encounter a variety of fonts: serif (e.g., **a**, **b**, **c**), sans-serif (e.g., **a**, **b**, **c**), and even cursive (e.g., *a*, *b*, *c*). To identify letters, they must understand that an *A* in, for example, Courier font looks different from the same letter in Typewriter font, but that both fonts represent the same letter. This activity builds their familiarity with multiple representations of graphemes in print, including cursive.

HOW: The script below serves to jumpstart your directions and conversation. The **T** is teacher-directed language, and the **S** indicates what students do.

T: Look at this word. It is *bridge*. Say it with me.

S: *bridge*

T: Let's look at the different letters in this word. Sometimes there is only one way to make a letter; for example, the letter *i* looks the same across lots of different types. But the letter *g* might look different based on the font or handwriting. Here, the *g* has a hook at the bottom, but in other fonts it has a closed loop at the bottom—like in cursive. Though they look different, they all represent the same sound and have the same letter name. Can you find any other letters in the word *bridge* that might look different?

S: (Students share out any letters that have differing formats.)

T: Remember that even if they have a different appearance, the letter name and sound is still the same.

TIPS

- You might begin by showing students a single letter in a variety of fonts, which you can print out from your word-processing program or clip from magazines. Have students describe the differences in the letter's shapes and formats, reminding them that some letters vary greatly (such as *g*) and others don't (such as *o*).
- If your students have not had explicit instruction in or exposure to cursive, focus on various fonts. But if they are familiar with cursive, be sure to include letters written in it.

Step 2: Segment & Spell

STEP 2

These are the menu options for Segment & Spell, the step in the routine in which students analyze the sounds of the word and match the appropriate letters to those sounds. As a result, they make grapheme (letter)-phoneme (sound) connections that build their knowledge of spelling patterns.

Count It, Box It, Spell It

Materials

- Word written so students can see it
- Count and Box Letters student copies (Appendix B)
- Set of 4–5 small manipulatives, such as coins, tokens, small blocks

WHAT: Elkonin Boxes (or simply "sound boxes") are a widely used approach to segmenting sounds in words and matching the letters to the sounds to spell words (Keesey et al., 2015).

HOW: The script below serves to jumpstart your directions and conversation. The **T** is teacher-directed language, and the **S** indicates what students do. Place some pennies in the circle at the top of the page.

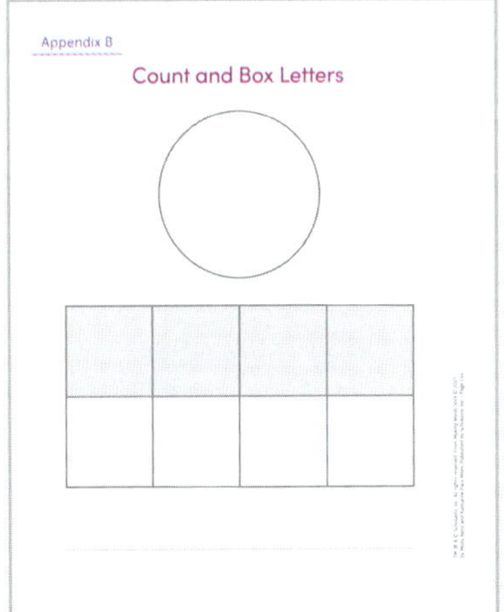

T: The pennies in this circle are going to represent sounds in words. I will slide one penny into the top row of gray boxes to represent each sound I hear in a word. Look at this word. It is *bridge*. Say it.

S: *bridge*

T: Now watch as I slide a penny for each sound in the word *bridge* into the top row of gray boxes, which are our sound boxes. (Says a sound in the word and moves a penny into each box.) Watch as I say each sound and write the letter or letter unit that represents that sound in the word. (Says each sound and writes the letter(s) that represent the sound in the box below the sound boxes.) Now I write the word on the line, and I read the word. Your turn. Say the word again.

S: *bridge*

T: Now move a penny into each of the top row of gray sound boxes for each of the sounds you hear in *bridge*.

S: (Students move a penny for each sound.)

T: Now write the letter or letters that represent each sound in the word in the bottom row of boxes.

S: (Students write the letter(s) that represent each sound in the word.)

T: Now write the word on the line and read it.

S: (Students write the word on the line and read it.)

TIP

Change the manipulatives you use as often as possible—bingo stampers, Unifix® cubes, LEGO® blocks, checkers, etc.—to keep the activity fresh.

Count It, Spell It Three Ways

Materials

- Word written so students can see it
- Writing materials

WHAT: Our aim here is to provide students more than one opportunity to practice the letter formation of each letter, and to map the sounds to the letters as they rewrite the word. Simply spelling the word has been shown to be an effective approach to storing words in memory (Colenbrander et al., 2022).

HOW: The script below serves to jumpstart your directions and conversation. The **T** is teacher-directed language, and the **S** indicates what students do.

T: Look at this word. It is *bridge*. Say it.

S: *bridge*

T: Count the sounds you hear in *bridge*.

S: /b/ /r/ /i/ /j/

TIP

Get creative by using sand, fingerpaints, shaving cream on trays, sidewalk chalk, glitter-glue pens, alphabet stickers, pipe cleaners, etc. Sometimes simply giving students more engaging writing instruments is a real motivator!

T: Now spell the word *bridge*. Be sure to represent each sound you hear.

S: (Students spell the word.)

T: Look at my spelling. Let's say the letters together. Make any corrections.

S: (Students correct their spellings as the teacher and students spell the word out loud.)

T: Now spell the word in three different sizes (S, M, L)/in different colors/in different directions (sideways, upside down, slanted)/in different handwriting at the bottom of your paper.

S: (Students write the word correctly in three different ways.)

Count It, Line It, Spell It

Materials

- Word written so students can see it

WHAT: This activity leans into the basic spelling approach that Colenbrander and colleagues (2022) found to be effective. However, prior to spelling the word, students underline the letters that make up each sound in it and say each sound.

HOW: The script below serves to jumpstart your directions and conversation. The **T** is teacher-directed language, and the **S** indicates what students do.

T: Look at this word. It is *bridge*. Say it.

S: *bridge*

T: Count the sounds in *bridge*.

S: (Students hold up a finger as they say each sound in *bridge*: /b/ /r/ /i/ /j/—four fingers total.)

T: Watch as I underline each letter or letter unit as I say the sounds in *bridge*. (Says /b/ and underlines the *b*. Then says /r/ and underlines the *r*, making sure it is not attached to the *b*. Says /i/

TIPS

- The approach to matching the letters and the sounds they make can be used for regularly and irregularly spelled words. For irregularly spelled words, it can be an opportunity to reconcile the sounds in the word with the unexpected spelling of those sounds.
- Using a mnemonic or memory pronunciation of a word as you spell it may be a good way to secure the irregular spelling of the word in memory—for example, pronouncing *chocolate* as *choc-o-late* as you spell it, or *many* as *m-a-n-y*.

and underlines the *i*, making sure it is not attached to the *r*. Says /j/ and underlines the *-dge*, making sure it is not attached to the *i*. There should be four short lines under each letter or letter unit.) Now it's your turn.

S: (Students say each sound in *bridge* and underline the letter(s) that represent each sound.)

T: Now underline the entire word as you say the word.

S: (Students draw a long line under the word as they say *bridge*.)

Step 3: Study & Suss Out

These are the menu options for Study & Suss Out, the step in the routine in which students activate the meaning of the word. Our goal is for them to understand the definition, identify possible multiple meanings, and correct usage/application of the word.

Word Web It

Materials

- Word written so students can see it
- Word Web (Appendix F)

WHAT: In his explanation of lexical quality hypothesis, Perfetti (2007) explains that our rapid and accurate retrieval of a word is facilitated by a deep knowledge of that word—its meaning, uses, related components, contexts, etc. A word web is a graphic organizer that builds such knowledge. It contains a focus word in the center and related words, phrases, examples, and contexts radiating from it. As students create them, they connect a new word to other words they might know and explore the word well beyond its meaning.

HOW: The script below serves to jumpstart your directions and conversation. The **T** is teacher-directed language, and the **S** indicates what students do.

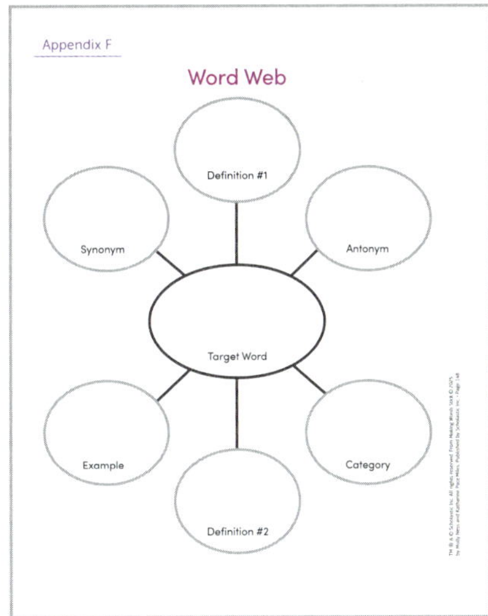

T: The word is *bridge*. I'm going to write that word into the middle of my web here because it's the word we are focusing on. In the other spaces, I'm going to put things related to that word. Please join me by writing *bridge* in the middle of your web.

S: (Students write *bridge* in the middle of their web.)

T: Now let's go to the Definition #1 bubble. Can someone tell me the most common definition of *bridge*, which is a noun?

S: (Students provide a definition.)

T: Is there another definition of *bridge* as a verb that we can write in the Definition #2 bubble?

S: (Students provide a definition.)

T: In the Synonym bubble, we are going to write words that are similar to *bridge*. Turn and talk to your neighbor about other words that are related to Definition #1. (Waits, and then asks for examples.) Who would like to share?

S: *platform, arch, overpass*

T: Now work with your partner on synonyms for Definition #2. (Waits, and then asks for examples.) Who would like to share?

S: *connect, link, join, attach*

T: Okay, now let's move to Sentence for Definition #1. Please write a sentence that uses *bridge* as a noun. (Waits, and then asks for examples.) Who would like to share?

S: (Students share their sentences.)

T: Now go to the Sentence for Definition #2 bubble. Please write a sentence that uses *bridge* as a verb. (Waits, and then asks for examples.) Who would like to share?

S: (Students share their sentences.)

TIPS

- In our script, we focus on definitions of words, but you might start with characteristics of words and/or associations with one version of the word. For instance, to build understanding of the *bridge* that cars travel across, students might list things that jump to mind when they think of that kind of bridge—cars, tolls, examples of well-known bridges in their area (e.g., the Golden Gate Bridge or London Bridge from the popular nursery rhyme). This builds students' understanding of one version of the word by exploring its connections, associations, examples, characteristics, etc.
- There are tons of word webs available for free! The key is to use one that works well for your chosen word. Some words have antonyms, others don't. Some words can be easily captured in a drawing, others can't. Choose your web wisely.

Word Expert Card It

Materials

- Word written so students can see it
- Word Expert Card (Appendix G)

WHAT: With a Word Expert Card, students delight in capturing a word's meaning in an illustration. Specifically, they explore a word in four quadrants: the word itself, the word's definition, an illustration of the word, and the word in a sentence (Landsdown, 1991; Richek, 2005). This kind of visual representation of a word is particularly useful to multilingual learners.

HOW: The script below serves to jumpstart your directions and conversation. The **T** is teacher-directed language, and the **S** indicates what students do.

T: Notice how my page has four boxes, or quadrants. In this quadrant, I'm going to write the word *bridge*. Go ahead and write the word in your box.

S: (Students write the word *bridge* in the appropriate box.)

T: Next, we are going to write down the definition of the word into this second box. A *bridge* is a structure that people cross to go over something, like water. Let's write that down in our boxes.

S: (Students write the definition for *bridge* in the appropriate box.)

T: Next, I'm going to do a quick pencil sketch of the word. Watch as I draw the water underneath and a bridge going over the water so cars can cross. (Draws a pencil sketch of *bridge*.) Now it's your turn to draw a bridge. You can make yours look like mine, or you can add different details. We will draw for two minutes.

S: (Students sketch an image of *bridge* into the appropriate box.)

T: Now to finish up my word expert card, I want to use the word in a sentence that proves I really know what the word means. My sentence is "The traffic was very heavy as the cars crossed the bridge." Now turn to your neighbor and

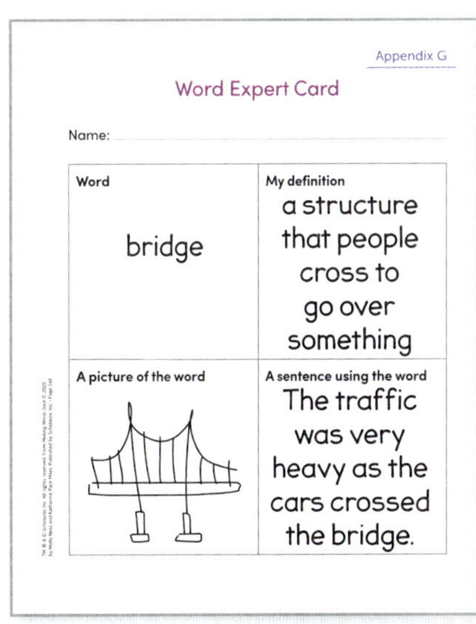
Appendix G

Word Expert Card

Name:

Word	My definition
bridge	a structure that people cross to go over something
A picture of the word	**A sentence using the word**
	The traffic was very heavy as the cars crossed the bridge.

write a sentence for *bridge*. Once you've got that sentence, you can write it in the last box.

S: (Students talk to a partner to come up with a sentence and write the sentence or a teacher-supplied sentence in the appropriate box.)

T: Our cards are now finished. Go ahead and read your sentence to your neighbor and explain the picture that you illustrated.

TIPS

- The sketch does not need to be sophisticated—a simple pencil sketch works!
- There are many formats for this, including the template we provide. Older students might use blank index cards or simply fold a piece of paper into quadrants.
- If students get overly involved in the illustration of the word, set a timer. If you assign homework, have students do the illustration at home. Older students might use digital imagery, such as Google Images or clip art, to represent the word.
- Ask students to explain their thinking behind their images. Not only does this encourage oral language, but it builds their metacognition and provides insight into their thinking. This is also a great vocabulary assessment activity!

Paint Swatch It

Materials

- Word written so students can see it
- Paint swatch cards taken from hardware stores. If none are available, digital images will work too!

WHAT: Our aim here is to build students' vocabulary depth, the quality of knowledge about words (Hadley et al., 2018). This activity, from our colleague Esther Friedman, helps students examine the semantic relations between words, using gradations of color for inspiration. Gather paint samples from your local home-improvement store and remind children that the more saturated the color, the more intense the level of the word.

HOW: The script below serves to jumpstart your directions and conversation. The **T** is teacher-directed language, and the **S** indicates what students do.

T: We've been working with the word *bridge* when it's used as a noun. But *bridge* can also be a verb, or an action word. When *bridge* is a verb, it means to make a bridge across things, or to connect things.

For example, if I wanted to cross over a stream I could say, "The fallen log bridged the stream so I could get to the other side."

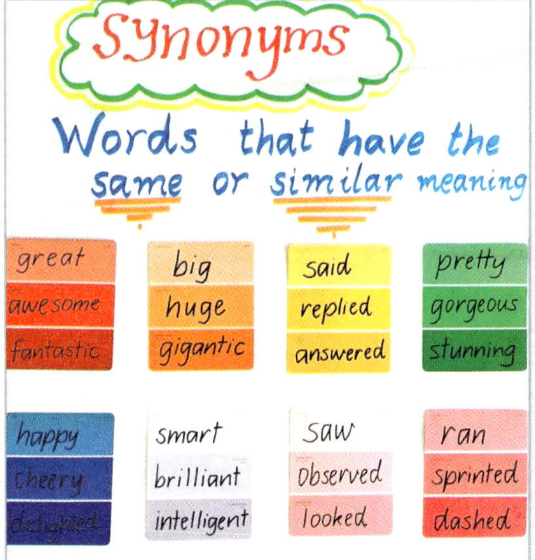

T: The different levels of colors on the paint swatches represent different levels of meaning or variations of the same word. The deeper the color, the more advanced or sophisticated the level of the word is. So I need to think of words that are related to *bridge*. Right away, I think of the words *link* and *connect*. I'm going to choose the word that's weakest, *connect*, for the lightest color on my swatch. It could mean just barely making things meet. Next could be *link*, it means joining two things—like links in a chain link fence.

S: (Students write the words in their paint swatches)

T: Now if I'm thinking about levels of the word, then our word *bridge* would go above *link* and *connect*—since it's a deeper or more advanced word that means to link or connect. Let's write that word in.

S: (Students write *bridge* in the third level of their paint swatches.)

T: I'm going to think of an even more advanced word that's related to *bridge*, *connect*, and *link*, and it will go at the top of our paint swatch. The word is *span*. I'll write it for you to see, and you can add it to your swatch.

S: (Students write the word in their paint swatches.)

T: My paint swatch shows me that all of these words are related or connected, but there are different levels of words.

TIPS

- Start with three levels of colors to limit the number of words you generate. As students master the activity, increase the number of levels.
- Jumpstart your thinking—and your students' thinking—with the thesaurus. Think aloud as you look up a word. Many students may not be familiar with the thesaurus, and this activity helps them get familiar with it!

STEP 3

Study & Suss Out

Word Parts

Materials

- Word written so students can see it
- Word Part Organizer (Appendix C)

WHAT: Let's build our students' understanding of morphology, or how meaningful parts of a word come together to create the word's overall meaning. A review of research (Bowers et al., 2010) indicated that morphological instruction benefits younger readers, particularly less skilled readers.

HOW: The script below serves to jumpstart your directions and conversation. The **T** is teacher-directed language, and the **S** indicates what students do.

T: We have been working with the word *bridge*. We've looked at it as a noun and a verb. Now I'm going to add different word parts to *bridge* to connect it to new words: *bridging* and *bridged* and *bridges*. Say these words as I point to them.

S: *bridging*, *bridged*, *bridges*

T: Write *bridge* in the box.

S: (Students write *bridge* in the box.)

T: Write the definitions below *bridge*.

S: (Students write the definitions.)

T: Confirms the definition with students' help.

T: Now let's add the ending *-ing* in the box on the right side.

S: (Students write *bridging* in the box on the right.)

T: When we add *-ing* to a word, it turns the word into a present-tense action. So what would *bridging* mean?

Appendix C

Word Part Organizer

Target Word	+ Ending =	

Target Word	+ Ending =	

Target Word	+ Ending =	

Target Word	+ Ending =	

TIP

Most second and third graders are ready to read and write simple prefixes and suffixes. Be sure to explain their meanings so students can apply that knowledge to other words.

S: (Students share ideas about what *bridging* means.)

T: Write the definition in your own words under *bridging*. (Repeat for *bridged* and *bridges*)

Know Its Many Meanings

Materials

- A word with multiple meanings written so students can see it

WHAT: Being able to use a word accurately and appropriately in a sentence is the ultimate goal of vocabulary learning! For this activity, give students a word with multiple meanings and then have them write sentences that demonstrate their understanding of each meaning. This instructional recommendation builds children's application of multiple-meaning words (Booton et al., 2022).

HOW: The script below serves to jumpstart your directions and conversation. The **T** is teacher-directed language, and the **S** indicates what students do.

T: The word is *bridge*. This word has more than one meaning as a noun, and it can be a verb like we discussed. Let's talk about its different meanings when it is a noun. We've discussed that it can be a structure that connects one thing to another, like a bridge that goes over a river so cars can cross. Here are other ways we can use *bridge*.

- The bridge of your nose, which is the upper part in between your eyes
- Something that dentists use to replace missing teeth
- A card game that people play in groups of four
- A section in a piece of music that connects one part to another

T: Listen as I use *bridge* in a sentence; I'll use the meaning of *bridge* that relates to dentists. The dentist used a bridge to fix the patient's missing teeth.

T: Now together, let's write a sentence for the *bridge* that is a part of music. Can you help me think of a sentence?

S: (Students help teacher think of a sentence.)

T: Now there are two other types of *bridge*. Let's see if the partner sitting closest to the door can come up with a sentence using the word *bridge* as it relates to a part of your nose. Go ahead and try.

S: (Partner 1 shares a sentence referring to the bridge of your nose.)

T: Now the other partner will come up with a sentence for the *bridge* that is a card game. Take a minute to think of a juicy sentence with details. Okay, Partner 2, share your sentence.

S: (Partner 2 shares a sentence referring to the card game called *Bridge*.)

T: Who would like to nominate their partner to share their sentence because it had so many juicy details?

T: When you get back to your seats, choose one way to use *bridge* in a sentence and write it down. You may use a sentence that you heard or a sentence that you gave.

TIP
As children move up in grade level, it's easy to prioritize reading and writing over speaking and listening. But it is still critical to develop oral-language skills, especially for English language learners.

Word Ladder It

Materials

- Word Ladder (Appendix H)

WHAT: In this activity, students consider the spelling and meaning of a word and how a small change to its spelling can radically change its meaning. In addition to decoding and spelling skills, this activity builds vocabulary and phonemic awareness.

HOW: The script below serves to jumpstart your directions and conversation. The **T** is teacher-directed language, and the **S** indicates what students do.

T: Let's start at the bottom of this ladder. If I asked you to write the word that means "a structure that connects two pieces of land," you would write the word *bridge,* so please do that.

S: (Students write *bridge*.)

T: Next clue: Delete one letter to change the meaning to "a long, narrow raised piece of land."

S: (Students write *ridge*)

T: Next clue: Delete one letter and change one letter to change the meaning to "the end of a surface."

S: (Students write *edge*.)

T: Next clue: Add a letter to mean "a row of bushes."

S: (Students write *hedge*.)

T: Last clue: Change a letter to make the word that means "a piece of wood that is narrow on one side and thick on the other and is used to shove between two objects or things."

S: (Students write *wedge*.)

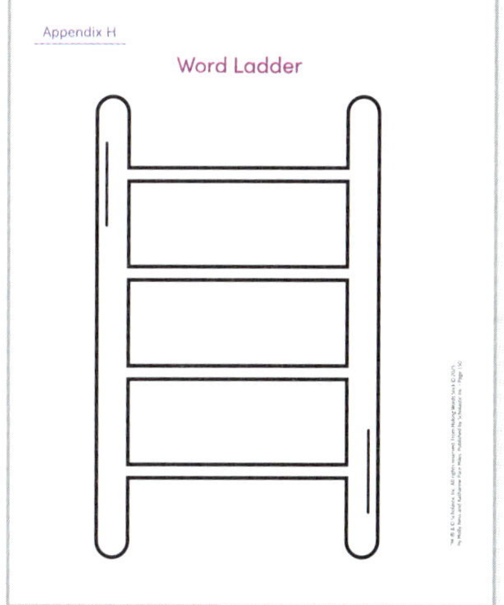

TIP

This activity is especially fun to do in pairs or small groups as a competition to determine "teams" that can figure out words based on the clues.

Study & Suss Out: Function Words

There are many words that can't be defined or depicted—you need to use them to understand their meanings (Miles & Ehri, 2017; Miles et al., 2018). Function words, such as *there*, *were*, and *its*, are among them. Because function words are tricky to define, they need a specific type of activity for Study & Suss Out. In other words, use Steps 1, 2, and 4 for function words, but the following substitutions for Step 3.

Hear It, Use It

Materials

- Word written so students can see it
- A set of word cards in small plastic bags that form a sentence and a question for each student. See guidelines below.

WHAT: Remember that function words have little meaning but signal grammatical relationships, hold semantic importance, and are the connective tissue of sentences (Miles et al., 2018). In this activity, students listen for the word in a sentence read to them and then create their own sentences containing the word (Ehri & Wilce, 1985). Thus, the activity provides exposure to the function words, in addition to application.

HOW: The script below serves to jumpstart your directions and conversation. The **T** is teacher-directed language, and the **S** indicates what students do.

Watch Molly carry out the routine for a function word.

T: Look at this word. It is *across*. Say it.

S: *across*.

T: Now listen to how the word *across* is used in this sentence, "My best friend lives across the street from me."

T: In this baggie, you have words that create a sentence. Please put them in order on your desk to create a sentence. There may be some words that you don't use. Just put those over to the side.

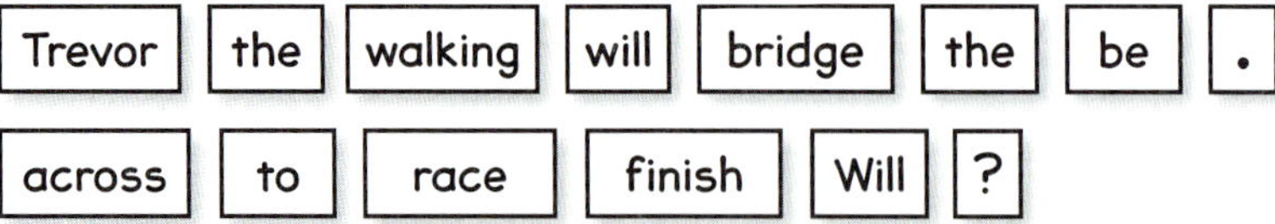

S: (Students empty their baggies and arrange the words in a sentence, including the punctuation card with a period on it.)

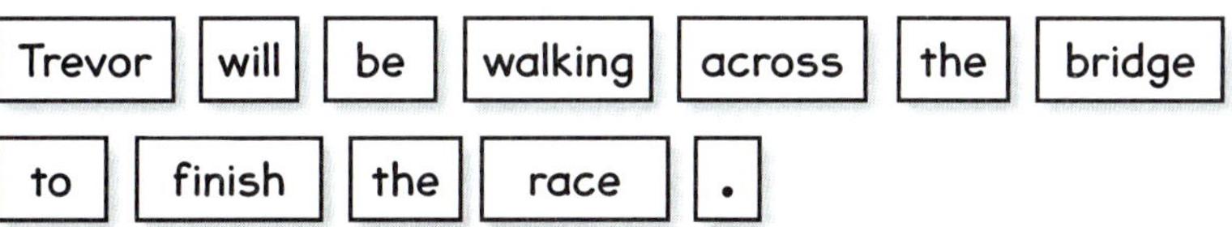

T: Read your sentence to a neighbor.

S: (Students read their sentence and make any corrections.)

T: Now create a question using the words. You may leave out different words this time.

S: (Students rearrange the words to create a question, including the punctuation card with a question mark on it.)

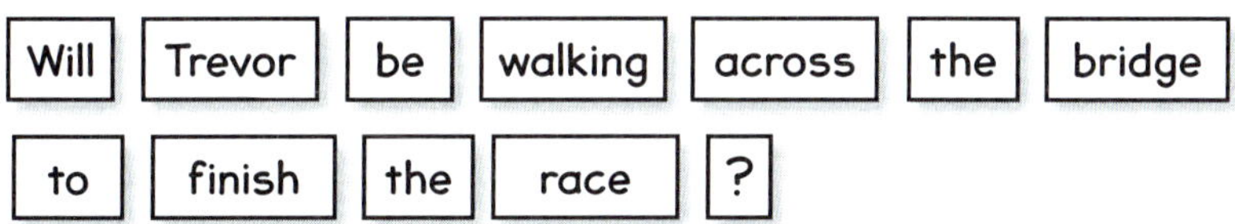

T: Read your question to a neighbor.

TIPS

- Students can make longer or shorter sentences depending on their sentence generation abilities.
- When working with multilingual learners, it may be helpful to provide the placement of two of the word cards in the sequence (beginning, middle, or end) to get the students going.

Choose It, Use It

Materials

- A paragraph from a grade-level text with function words omitted or redacted

WHAT: In a 2018 article, Katie and colleagues (Miles et al., 2018) wrote that function words "rely on surrounding words for their meaning" and that they are particularly difficult to learn in isolation—when no information is available about the meaning or usage of the word. Logically, our function word instruction should focus more on usage and application, as in this activity. For this activity, students read a text with function words redacted. From there, they must think about possible words and incorporate them in a way that makes the text make sense.

HOW: The script below serves to jumpstart your directions and conversation. The **T** is teacher-directed language, and the **S** indicates what students do.

> **T:** We are going to complete a paragraph that is missing a bunch of words! Read this to yourself and circle the word that makes the most sense when you come to the blank. Go ahead.
>
> **S:** (Students begin reading the paragraph silently and circling the appropriate missing words.)

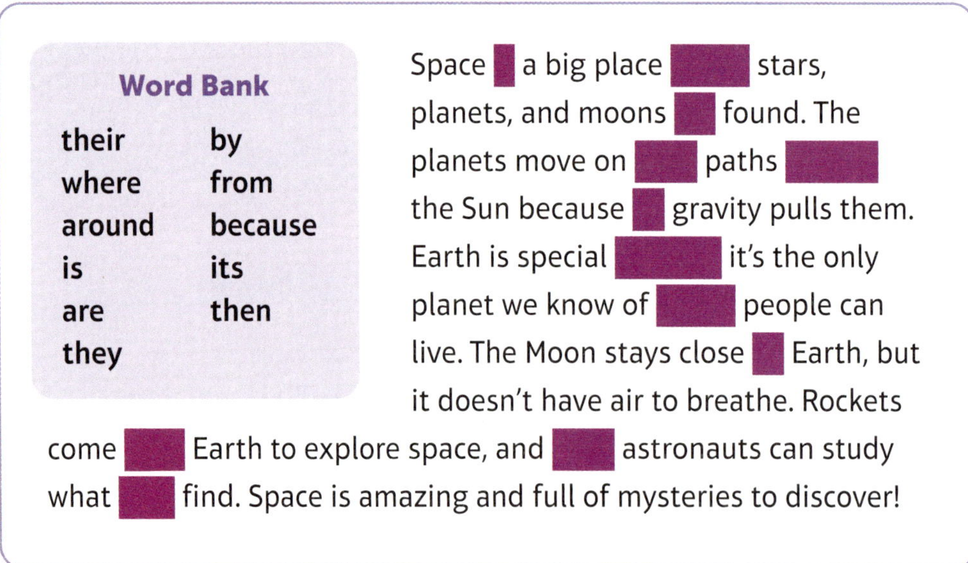

Word Bank

their	by
where	from
around	because
is	its
are	then
they	

Space ____ a big place ____ stars, planets, and moons ____ found. The planets move on ____ paths ____ the Sun because ____ gravity pulls them. Earth is special ____ it's the only planet we know of ____ people can live. The Moon stays close ____ Earth, but it doesn't have air to breathe. Rockets come ____ Earth to explore space, and ____ astronauts can study what ____ find. Space is amazing and full of mysteries to discover!

T: Now whisper-read your paragraph and see if you need to make any adjustments.

S: (Students whisper-read their paragraphs.)

T: Now read your paragraph to a partner. Take turns and make any corrections.

S: (Students take turns reading their paragraphs to their partners.)

T: Now let's read our paragraphs altogether. Make any adjustments.

TIP

This is loosely related to the beloved game Mad Libs, so students might appreciate making a connection between this activity and that game. But instead of being silly, as students typically would be when playing Mad Libs, they should focus on accurate usage/application of words.

Step 4: Search & Stick

These are the menu options for Search & Stick, the step in the routine designed to help students automatically recognize the word. Our aim is immediate retrieval, efficiency, and connection to the word's use in text.

Hunt for It

Materials

- Grade-level text and/or decodable readers
- Small sticky notes
- Decodable and/or leveled text
- Magnifying glass (optional—just for fun!)

WHAT: It's not enough for us to help students recognize words in isolation. We must help them transfer—or extend—what we've taught them in word study to connected text (Bransford et al., 1999). This activity helps them to do just that.

HOW: The script below serves to jumpstart your directions and conversation. The **T** is teacher-directed language, and the **S** indicates what students do.

T: We have been working with the word *bridge*. This word has a beginning /br/ blend and a consonant cluster of /dge/. We are going to see if we can find those phonics patterns in other books that we read. When you read words that have either one of those patterns, place a sticky note next to it.

S: (Students begin reading the book, and at the end of reading a sentence, they go back to place a sticky note on the page where they've located an appropriate word.)

T: Nice job reading the book. Now, flip through and remove all the sticky notes while you read each underlined word.

S: (Students read all similar words as they remove the sticky notes.)

TIPS

- Model this activity by projecting a preselected page from a text. Demonstrate how to scan and mark the page when you encounter appropriate words. Remind students that they are not hunting for the exact word, but rather words that contain the same phonics pattern.
- Differentiate by narrowing the number of features for which students search. Encourage students who are ready for it to search for two patterns. Some students might benefit more from looking for just the /br/ blend.
- Other students might benefit more from transcribing the words that they've found while highlighting and/or circling the target phonics pattern within the word.

Word Sorts

Materials

- Small plastic bags
- Sets of 5–10 words with the new spelling pattern (e.g., *-dge*) and 5–10 review words with a different spelling pattern (e.g., *j*)

WHAT: Word sorts allow students to compare and contrast how similar sounds may be spelled with different phonetic concepts. Here we draw students' attention to two spelling patterns. Those patterns can represent the same sound (/j/ spelled *j*, *g*, or *dge*) or two easily confused spelling patterns that represent different sounds (*or* vs. *ar*).

HOW: The script below serves to jumpstart your directions and conversation. The **T** is teacher-directed language, and the **S** indicates what students do.

T: We have been working on the word *bridge*. Now sort this baggie of words into two columns: words that end in *-ge* and words that end in *-dge*.

T: Since words in English never end in *j*, if you hear /j/ at the end of a word it must be *-dge* or *-ge*. The spelling *-dge* is used right after a short vowel, but the /j/ sound after any other sound is spelled with *-ge*.

S: (Students dump the baggie onto the table, find the colorful heading strips, and sort the words into the two piles: *bridge, hedge, ledge, fridge, badge, wedge, lodge, judge, nudge, age, huge, cage, page, rage, large, change, orange, village.*)

T: Now quietly read down both columns.

S: (Students quietly read the words in the columns.)

T: Now read these words to your partner. Partner 1 reads column 1, and Partner 2 reads column 2. Then switch columns.

S: (Students take turns reading aloud down each column.)

T: Now who can explain the spelling pattern when you hear the /j/ sound in a word?

TIP
Be sure students read the words aloud after they sort them into two columns to help them process and analyze the spelling-to-pronunciation connection. You might have them audio record themselves saying the words or use whisper phones!

Find Its Look-Alike

Materials

- Look-Alike Word Activity (Appendix I)

WHAT: In this activity, students pay very close attention to letter combinations in similarly spelled words to read them accurately and efficiently.

HOW: The script below serves to jumpstart your directions and conversation. The **T** is teacher-directed language, and the **S** indicates what students do.

T: We have been working on the word *bridge*. You will see that word and many other similarly spelled words on this chart. Your job is to slowly read the words aloud to a partner the first time, and then try to read them more swiftly on your second turn. Get ready, Partner 1.

S: (Partner 1 reads the chart of words accurately.)

T: Okay, now Partner 2 get ready.

S: (Partner 2 reads the chart of words accurately.)

T: Now Partner 1, it's your turn again. Try to read a little more swiftly this time, but you must remain accurate!

S: (Partner 1 reads the words.)

T: Partner 2, it's your turn to read a bit more swiftly while remaining accurate!

S: (Partner 2 reads the words.)

TIPS

- Have fun with this! Ask the reading partner to stand as if giving a presentation, while the other partner sits on the floor paying close attention to the reading partner's accuracy. You may even want to give the reading partner a fake microphone or other performance prop.
- You'll notice we don't suggest using a timer. That is intentional so that students prioritize accuracy over speed. If you feel strongly about timers, and your students can handle their use and competitive nature, go for it!

In Closing, Remember...

As students in the full-alphabetic phase begin their more dramatic literacy ascent, their reading and spelling becomes more efficient and accurate. Though students might face some turbulence along the way, they are closer to cruising at altitude—reading with efficiency and automaticity. The Making Words Stick menu moves second and third graders into more fluent reading, which assists with comprehension.

Terms to Remember	
Affix	One or more sounds or letters attached to the beginning or end of a word, base, or phrase or inserted within a word or base and serving to produce a derivative word or an inflectional form (prefixes and suffixes).
Elkonin Boxes	Tools for phonemic awareness and encoding instruction that contain a space, or "box," for each sound in a target word. They are sometimes referred to as "sound boxes."
Explicit Instruction	A teaching method that involves a teacher clearly demonstrating what students should do and how to do it. It's characterized by a high level of teacher-student interaction. The teacher's actions are clear, direct, and visible to all students.
Grapheme-Phoneme Connections	Letter-sound connections.
Homophone	A homophone is a word that sounds the same as another word but has a different meaning or spelling. Examples: flour/flower, knight/night, hour/our.
Multimodal	Multimodal literacy involves using multiple senses and modalities, such as visual, oral, linguistic, gestural, and spatial, to engage learners who have different learning styles.
Multisensory	Multisensory literacy is a teaching method that uses more than one sense at a time to help students learn to read. Instruction often includes elements that rely on visual, auditory, tactile, and kinesthetic stimuli. It is widely regarded as a more engaging and effective approach than instruction that involves engaging only one sense.
Prefix	A group of letters that is added to the beginning of a word to change its meaning. Examples: *re-*, *un-*, *dis-*.
Suffix	A group of letters added to the end of a word to change its meaning, grammatical function, or part of speech. Examples: *-ing*, *-tion*, *-er*.
Syllable Awareness	The ability to recognize, identify, and manipulate syllables within spoken words. Understanding how words can be broken down into smaller sound parts called *syllables* is a key foundational skill for reading multisyllabic words and is considered part of phonological awareness.
Systematic Instruction	A teaching method that organizes material in a logical order, building from simple to complex concepts and skills.
Word Web	A graphic organizer that builds knowledge about a word. It contains a focus word in the center and related words, phrases, examples, and contexts radiating from it.

CHAPTER 6

Making Words Stick in Grades 4 and 5

In upper-elementary classrooms, students should be at a cruising altitude with reading and spelling skills, based on their grade-level phonics scope and sequence. They should be soaring—with minimal turbulence—into reading more complex texts.

Consolidated Alphabetic Readers

Many fourth and fifth graders have transitioned from the full-alphabetic phase to the consolidated alphabetic phase, meaning they *are* using phonics knowledge regularly to decode words. So our focus turns to advanced phonetic concepts, such as affixes (prefixes, suffixes) and Greek and Latin word parts, to decode multisyllabic words and less common vowel patterns (*ey* for /a/, *ie* for /e/). Much of word study at this level focuses on morphology, the knowledge of meaningful word parts, including prefixes, suffixes, and/or root and base words (Foorman et al., 2016). By the end of fifth grade, students should be squarely in the consolidated alphabetic phase, reading and spelling complex multisyllabic words effortlessly.

One way divers and swimmers can stay safe fom Sharks is a chain mail suit. Chain mail is a suit that is made out of 400,000 tiny Stainless steel rings and protects divers from being hurt by a Shark bite. This detail Shows that Small rings on a chain mail suit stops sharks teeth from biting through skin. But the diver will still be bruised. Chain mail was body armor that Knights wore in the middle Ages between the 5th and 16th centuries. It a mesh-like fabric that was flexible and protected them against jabs from Swords and arrows. Now chain mail suits are used for diving and to protect divers from Shark bites. On one diving trip Ron and Valerie

Did You Know?
Heidi Ann Mesmer (2024) reminds us that a morpheme is a meaning unit that may or may not stand alone. All words have at least one. Helping students find morphemes in words assists their decoding, spelling, and word identification accuracy (Vaughn et al., 2022)

What About Upper-Elementary Students Who Are Stuck?

Students who are stuck in the full- and partial-alphabetic phases—students who are not transferring phonics skills they've learned to their independent reading and writing—need word-analysis support multiple times a week. We must provide ongoing explicit support in intervention and remediation levels. Remember, our goal is automatic word identification with increasing rates of fluency so that students can devote cognitive energy to comprehension. In fact, when children do not have adequate word-recognition skills, their reading comprehension often doesn't improve, no matter how much direct support for comprehension they receive (Wang et al., 2024).

The Tension Between Reading and Spelling in Grades 4 and 5

Remember our analogy of reading and spelling as two opposing parts of a rubber band?

This metaphor reminds us that reading and spelling don't always develop at the same rate because reading is a recognition task, which is easier than the reproduction task of spelling. Sometimes students' word reading is much stronger than their spelling, so the rubber band is stretched further in one direction. At other points, the rubber band has equal tension to represent the synchrony of reading and spelling development.

Did You Know?
In upper-elementary classrooms, the texts that students encounter introduce approximately 20,000 new words, 90 percent of which are multisyllabic words (Kearns et al., 2016).

After learning a new phonetic concept, spelling may lag behind reading for a certain set of words, but after receiving spelling instruction, feedback, and ample practice opportunities, the tension between reading and spelling in the rubber band should release, and the skills should again be more closely aligned. We never want the tension to become so great that the rubber band snaps, meaning that the student no longer effectively transfers their phonetic elements knowledge that they use for reading to spelling.

When the rubber band is stretched too far in the direction of reading, with spelling lagging behind, students' writing fluency may suffer (Graham et al., 2002; Graham & Santangelo, 2014). We cannot assume

Benchmarks Related to Orthographic Mapping

Check for these behaviors and understandings to make sure your students are making steady gains.

GRADES 4 AND 5

- Applies grade-level phonics and morphological knowledge to read and spell multisyllabic words accurately.
- Identifies prefixes, suffixes, roots, or any word part to pronounce and spell words, and understand their meaning.
- Has a large corpus of high-frequency words (regularly or irregularly spelled) stored as sight words.

that students' spelling will improve on its own; many students require explicit, systematic instruction in applying grade-level phonetic patterns to spellings, as well as instruction in spelling rules. We suggest providing the following:

- A diagnostic assessment of spelling to determine where the breakdowns are happening (Seymour et al., 2024)
- Additional practice for spelling, with clear connections between phonics patterns and spelling
- Corrective feedback on spelling errors

The Instructional Routine for Grades 4 and 5

To make words stick in memory in upper-elementary classrooms, students need the same rigorous routine of saying the word, segmenting its sounds or parts, spelling it, understanding its meaning, and reading the word multiple times. Those rich levels of analysis clarify and strengthen connections between a word's spelling, pronunciation, and meaning—the key ingredients for orthographic mapping!

A Menu of Activities

The table on the next page provides a menu of activities for each step of our routine. Just as we suggested for grades K–3, when teaching a new word, select four activities—one from each column—and carry them out in the order of the routine. We encourage you to try all the activities; just remember, choose just one per column and follow the routine to ensure students are engaged and analyzing words deeply. Consider how you might mix and match activities from the menu.

Watch Katie carry out the grades 4–5 routine.

Did You Know? Wang, O'Reilly, and Sutherland (2024) point out a "decoding threshold"—the notion that if students don't attain a critical level of decoding skills, their reading comprehension suffers because they continue to divert too much energy to decoding. In fact, by the time they reach eighth grade, students should have retained "approximately 10,000 word-specific representations" (Ehri, 2005; Harris & Jacobson, 1982, in Stacey et al., 2020).

Choose one activity from each column and teach them in order.

 STEP 1 See & Say	 STEP 2 Segment & Spell	 STEP 3 Study & Suss Out	 STEP 4 Search & Stick
• See It, Say It, Scoop It • See It, Say It, Highlight It	• Count It, Cover It, Chunk Spell It, Check It • Count It, Box It	• Study Its Root • Frayer Model It **Function Words:** • Hear It, Use It • Choose It, Use It	• Word Part Chart It • Build It • Hunt for It

Place Your Order

Let's use this menu of activities to see how one teacher "places an order" for orthographic mapping in a fourth-grade classroom. Fourth-grade teacher Yasmine is teaching prefixes, so she used the following sequence:

Steps From the Routine	Activities Selected by Yasmine
See & Say	See It, Say It, Highlight It
Segment & Spell	Count It, Cover It, Chunk Spell It, Check It
Study & Suss Out	Frayer Model It
Search & Stick	Build It

Yasmine used this routine in each of her word-work/phonics lessons and added to the group of words with the target prefix *dis-* (*disconnect*, *disagree*, *dishonest*, *disorder*, *disable*, *disrespect*, *discount*, *dismantle*). When Yasmine moved onto a new prefix, *mis-* (*mistake*, *misunderstand*, *misprint*, *misspell*), she changed the routine to keep her explicit instruction fresh and engaging.

Steps From the Routine	Activities Selected by Yasmine
See & Say	See It, Say It, Scoop It
Segment & Spell	Count It, Box It
Study & Suss Out	Study Its Roots
Search & Stick	Word Part Chart It

Download lesson planning sheets.

Yasmine uses this routine in each of her small-group lessons and centers all week. With ample opportunity to see, say, segment sounds, spell, use, and read words with prefixes, her students stored the target words from her activities into long-term memory.

Activity Instructions and Scripts

On pages 123 to 139, we provide instructions and a short script for each activity for each step in the routine. The purpose of the scripts is to clarify the steps for each activity, as well as provide possible language to use with students. Feel free to modify our language, of course, to fit your own teaching style and goals and the needs of your students. Throughout the scripts, we use the target word *disruption* because of its rich morphemes.

Download all the student activity pages in this chapter.

The Many Meanings of *Disrupt*

Here are meanings of *disrupt* as a verb:

- To disturb or cause confusion. "Wasps disrupt class."
- To interrupt or break off. "Storms disrupt our telephone service."

Here's what happens to *disrupt* when inflected endings are added to it: *disrupts, disrupting, disrupted*.

Here are related words: *break, distract, heckle, sabotage, tear*

Word History: *Disrupt* comes from *disruptus*, a Latin word that means "to break apart or split." In Latin, there is a root (or word part), *rupt*, which means "to break." The English words *erupt*, which means "to break out or burst," and *rupture*, which means "to break open," also contain that root.

Our Recommended Phonics Scope and Sequence for Grades 4 and 5

Use it to select words for the activities.

More Word Study and Special Spellings

- Greek and Latin roots
- Schwa sound in multisyllabic words
- Suffixes (e.g., *-ness*, *-able*, *-ment*, *-tion*, *-sion*, *-ture*)

Step 1: See & Say

STEP
1

These are the menu options for See & Say, the step in the routine that helps students connect the written format of the word to its phonological representation, or pronunciation. Our goal is for students to break words into chunks, including prefixes, roots, and suffixes.

See It, Say It, Scoop It

Materials

- Multisyllabic affixed word (e.g., *nonsense* [prefix], *harmless* [suffix], or *unhelpful* [both]) written so students can see it

WHAT: The aim here is to draw students' awareness to the chunks in multisyllabic words, including those that contain affixes and roots. Students scoop a finger underneath each chunk of the word. As Devin Kearns and Victoria Whaley (2019) note, teaching students to locate base words and affixes is a particularly useful reading strategy for multisyllabic words.

TIP
Remind students that these chunks of words represent syllables, or units of pronunciation with a single vowel sound.

HOW: The script below serves to jumpstart your directions and conversation. The **T** is teacher-directed language, and the **S** indicates what students do.

> **T:** Look at this word. It is *disruption*. Say it.
>
> **S:** *disruption*
>
> **T:** The chunks in *disruption* are *dis-rup-tion*. Watch as I scoop my finger underneath each chunk. I pause very briefly after each chunk before I scoop the next one. Now you try.
>
> **S:** (Students scoop their fingers underneath the three chunks in *dis-rup-tion* as they say each chunk aloud.)

STEP 1

See & Say

See It, Say It, Highlight It

Materials

- Multisyllabic affixed word (e.g., *nonsense* [prefix], *harmless* [suffix], or *unhelpful* [both]) written so students can see it
- Highlighters of various colors

WHAT: Another way to help students recognize the prefixes, suffixes, and roots of words is to have them underline them, circle them, or highlight them. This draws their attention to the morphemes—or meaning units—in words (Archer et al., 2003).

HOW: The script below serves to jumpstart your directions and conversation. The **T** is teacher-directed language, and the **S** indicates what students do.

T: Look at this word. It is *disruption*. Say it.

S: *disruption*

T: The chunks in disruption are *dis-rup-tion*. Watch as I underline each chunk. See how I make sure there is a break in between each line to show the three different parts of the word? Now you try.

S: (Students underline the three chunks in *dis-rup-tion* as they say each chunk aloud.)

TIP

If using highlighters, have students use a variety of colors to mark the word: one color for a base word and others for the prefixes and suffixes.

Remember, some of the activities from grades 2 and 3 work just as effectively for grades 4 and 5. For instance, See It, Say It, Chin It (page 93) is a great way to give students additional practice in identifying and saying syllables in a multisyllabic word.

Step 2: Segment & Spell

These are the menu options for Segment & Spell, the step in the routine in which students analyze the sounds of the word and match the appropriate letters to those sounds. As a result, they make grapheme-phoneme connections that build their knowledge of spelling patterns.

Count It, Cover It, Chunk Spell It, Check It

Materials

- Multisyllabic affixed word (e.g., *nonsense* [prefix], *harmless* [suffix], or *unhelpful* [both] written so students can see it)

WHAT: Chunking not only helps students to read words but also to spell them. Breaking longer words into manageable parts makes the task of spelling multisyllabic words less daunting and more successful, as shown by Goodwin and Ahn (2013). In a 2022 WWC report, Sharon Vaughn and colleagues wrote that writing newly learned words helps embed them in a reader's memory.

HOW: The script below serves to jumpstart your directions and conversation. The **T** is teacher-directed language, and the **S** indicates what students do.

T: Look at this word. It is *disruption*. Say it.

S: *disruption*

T: Count the number of syllables you hear in the word.

S: *dis-rup-tion*, three

T: I am going to cover my board. First, draw a line for each syllable in the word.

S: (Students draw three lines on the paper.)

T: Now write each syllable as you say it out loud.

S: (Students spell *dis-rup-tion.*)

T: Now let's check one syllable at a time.

S: (Students check their work as teacher uncovers each syllable.)

TIP

When students check their spellings and make adjustments in real time, they take ownership for their own error correction; spelling researchers refer to this as the "self-corrected test" (Gentry, 2004; Simonsen & Gunter, 2001).

STEP 2

Segment & Spell

Count It, Box It

Materials

- Multisyllabic affixed word (e.g., *nonsense* [prefix], *harmless* [suffix], or *unhelpful* [both]) written so students can see it
- Count and Box Syllables (Appendix E)
- A set of 3–4 small manipulatives, such as coins or tokens

WHAT: Often referred to as "Elkonin Boxes" (or simply as "sound boxes"), this widely-used approach helps students segment words into sounds and match letters to sounds (Keesey et al., 2015).

HOW: The script below serves to jumpstart your directions and conversation. The **T** is teacher-directed language, and the **S** indicates what students do.

T: Look at this word. It is *disruption*. Say it.

S: *disruption*

T: Watch as I put a penny for each syllable of the word in the top boxes. (Says a syllable in the word and moves a penny into each box.) Now watch as I say each syllable and write the letters that represent each sound in the syllable. (Says each syllable and writes the letters that represent the sounds in the box below each penny.) Now I write the word and read it. Your turn. Say the word again.

S: *disruption*

T: Now move a penny into each of the top boxes for the syllables you hear in *disruption*.

S: (Students move a penny for each syllable.)

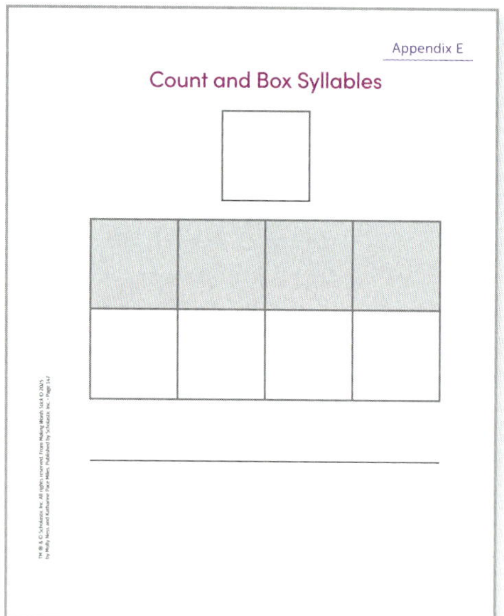

T: Now write the letters that represent each syllable in the word.

S: (Students write the letter(s) that represent each syllable in the word.)

T: Now write the word on the line and read it.

S: (Students write the word on the line and read it.)

TIP

Change the manipulatives you use as often as possible to keep the activity novel even though the steps and purpose stay the same.

Whether they're counting letters in kindergarten, letter sounds in grade 2, or syllables in grade 5, students learn so much from this Segment & Spell activity.

Step 3: Study & Suss Out

These are the menu options for Study & Suss Out, the step in the routine in which students activate the meaning of the word. Our goal is for them to understand the definition, possible multiple meanings, and correct usage and application of the word.

Study Its Root

Materials

- Multisyllabic affixed word (e.g., *nonsense* [prefix], *harmless* [suffix], or *unhelpful* [both]) written so students can see it
- Student-friendly dictionaries (online or print)
- Root Word Tree (Appendix J)

WHAT: A Root Word Tree builds students' word consciousness by drawing connections between words that share roots (Winters, 2009). As students examine roots of words and form new words with alternate prefixes and suffixes, they dive into morphology, the study of how meaningful parts of a word come together to create a word's meaning.

HOW: The script below serves to jumpstart your directions and conversation. The **T** is teacher-directed language, and the **S** indicates what students do.

T: Write the word *disruption* in the box at the top of the tree.

S: (Students write *disruption* in appropriate location.)

T: What is the prefix in *disruption*?

S: *dis-*

T: What is the suffix in *disruption*?

S: *-tion*

T: So what is the root of the word?

S: *rupt*

T: Yes, this comes from the Latin root *rumpere*, which means "to break." Fill in this information at the bottom of the tree. In English, *rupt* means "to break." (Writes information on the board.)

S: (Students fill in the bottom of the chart.)

T: Now work with a partner to fill in the tree with other words that have the same root: *rupt*. You will need to do some dictionary digging or internet searching. Be sure to read the definition of the new words you add.

S: (Students fill in the tree with *abrupt*, *erupt*, *interrupt*, *rupture*, *corruption*.)

TIP

Root Word Trees requires a quick lookup of words in an online or traditional dictionary. Make sure students understand the meanings of words they find.

Frayer Model It

Materials

- Multisyllabic affixed word (e.g., *nonsense* [prefix], *harmless* [suffix], or *unhelpful* [both]) written so students can see it
- Template for Frayer Model (Appendix K)

WHAT: Researcher Charles Perfetti (2007) argues that to retrieve a word rapidly and accurately, we need to know that word deeply—its meaning, usages, typical contexts, and so forth. Loosely related to the Word Expert Cards (see Chapter 5), a Frayer Model (Frayer et al., 1969; Peters, 1974) builds lexical quality by having students explore a word in four quadrants: the word itself, characteristics of the word, examples of the word, and non-examples of the word.

HOW: The script below serves to jumpstart your directions and conversation. The **T** is teacher-directed language, and the **S** indicates what students do.

T: Notice how my page has four boxes, or quadrants. In the center, I'm going to write the word *disruption*. Go ahead and write the word on your page.

S: (Students write the word *disruption* in the appropriate location.)

T: Next we are going to write down the definition of the word into this top box. A *disruption* is a disturbance or problem which interrupts something. Let's write that down in our boxes.

S: (Students write the definition for *disruption* into the appropriate box.)

T: Next, I'm going to think of characteristics, or descriptions, of our word. I'm looking for words or short phrases to describe the word *disruption*. So if our class were working quietly, a loud noise would be a *disruption*. Sometimes *disruptions* are a surprise, so I could

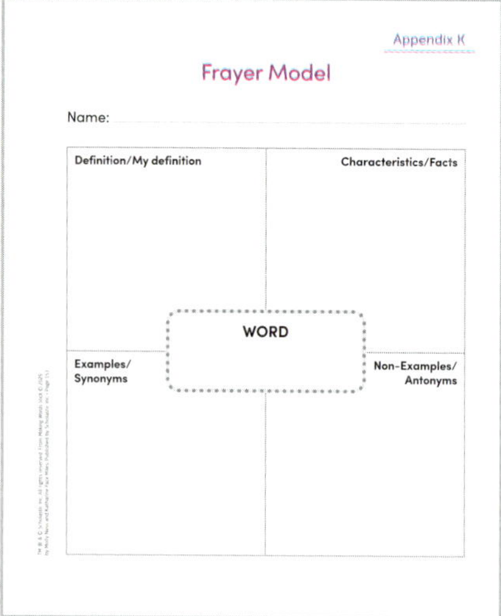

write "unexpected" as a characteristic. I could even write "messes things up" because disruptions are often inconvenient. I'm going to write all of these ideas in my Characteristics box, and you can do the same.

S: (Students complete Characteristics box.)

T: Our next job is to complete the Examples or Synonyms box. My work here is to think of an instance that is an example of *disruption*—like a fire alarm during class. Bad behavior can also be a *disruption*, as it might interrupt our focus if we are working. There are even examples of weather being a *disruption*, like if a rainstorm interrupted outdoor recess. Let's write all of these down in our third box.

S: (Students complete third box.)

T: Now to finish up my Frayer Model, I want to think of non-examples or antonyms of our word *disruption*. Remember that I can use real-life examples or short phrases. So if things are going as usual without a *disruption*, we might say that everything is stable or there is stability. Some other antonyms of *disruption* are *order* and *quiet*, because nothing is getting disrupted. Let's put those ideas into our last box.

S: (Students fill in the appropriate box.)

T: Our cards are now finished. Go ahead and read your boxes to your neighbor and explain the examples and non-examples you've come up with.

TIPS

- Encourage students to generate examples and non-examples based on their interests. For instance, if the word is *captivate*, they might choose Taylor Swift as an example and write a sentence like this: The pop star has captivated audiences around the globe!
- If the term *characteristics* is not familiar to students, you might use *descriptions* or "what it's like" as an alternative.

Study & Suss Out: Function Words

Did you know there are many words that can't be defined or depicted? They're function words, such as *which*, *how*, and *their*, and they are essential in holding space in sentences (Miles & Ehri, 2017; Miles et al., 2018). Because function words are tricky to define, they need a specific type of activity for Study & Suss Out. In other words, use Steps 1, 2, and 4 for function words, but the following substitutions for Step 3.

Hear It, Use It

Materials

- Word written so students can see it
- A set of word cards in small plastic bags that form a sentence and a question for each student. See guidelines below.

WHAT: Remember that function words have little meaning but signal grammatical relationships, hold semantic importance, and are the connective tissue of sentences (Miles et al., 2018). In this activity, we have students listen for the word in a sentence read to them, and then they create their own sentences containing the word (Ehri & Wilce, 1985). Thus, the activity provides exposure to the function words, in addition to application.

HOW: The script below serves to jumpstart your directions and conversation. The **T** is teacher-directed language, and the **S** indicates what students do.

T: Look at this word. It is *whether*. Say it.

S: *whether*.

T: This is a homophone of the word *weather*. These two words sound the same but are spelled differently and have different meanings. You know what *weather* means, but the other *whether* is not a word that can be easily defined.

Watch Molly carry out the routine for a function word.

T: There are words in this baggie, including the new word *whether*, that create a sentence. Please put them in order on your desk to create a sentence. There may be some words that you don't use. Just put those over to the side.

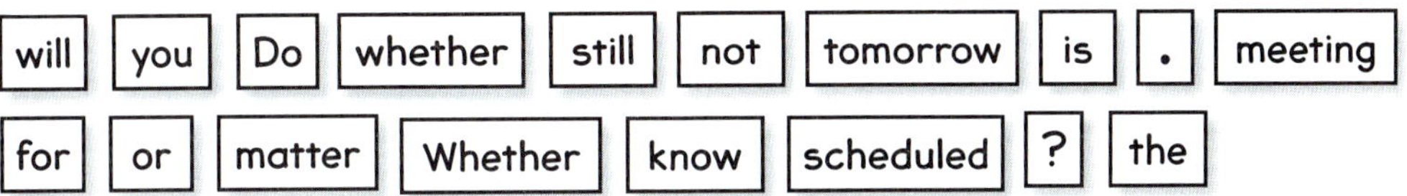

S: (Students empty their baggies and arrange the words in a sentence, including the punctuation card with a period on it.)

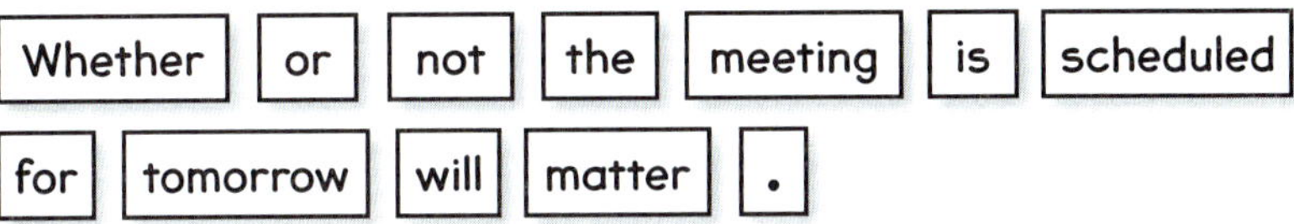

T: Read your sentence to a neighbor.

S: (Students read their sentences and make any corrections.)

T: Now grab the question mark card. Create a question using the words. You may have different words that are left out this time.

S: (Students rearrange the words to create a question, including the punctuation card with a question mark on it.)

T: Read your question to a neighbor.

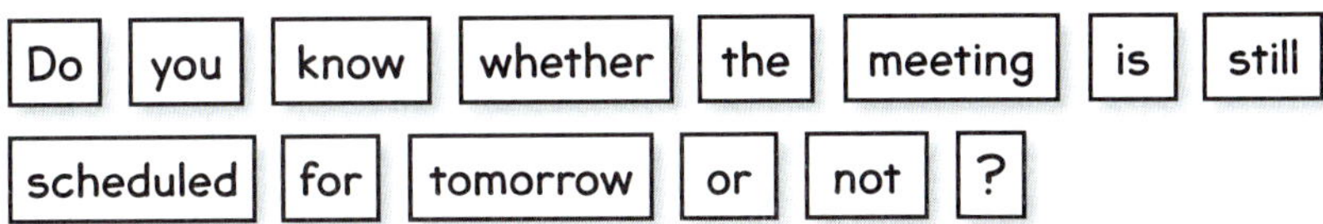

TIP

Students can make longer or shorter sentences depending on their sentence-generation abilities.

STEP 3

Study & Suss Out

Choose It, Use It

Materials

- A paragraph with function words omitted

WHAT: In a 2018 article, Katie and colleagues (Miles et al., 2018) wrote that function words "rely on surrounding words for their meaning" and that they are particularly difficult to learn in isolation—when no information is available about the meaning or usage of the word. Logically, our function word instruction should focus more on usage and application, as in this activity. Here we ask students to read a text with function words intentionally omitted, and then incorporate words into the text in a way that makes sense.

HOW: The script below serves to jumpstart your directions and conversation. The **T** is teacher-directed language, and the **S** indicates what students do.

T: We are going to complete a paragraph that is missing a bunch of words! Read this to yourself and circle the word that makes the most sense when you come to the blank. Go ahead.

Word Bank

they're
under
what
where
which
with

Plants are living things that grow in soil. They need water, sunlight, and air to live. Their roots grow ______ the ground, where they take in water and nutrients. Leaves use sunlight to make food, and ______ very important for the plant's health. If you ever wonder ______ plants get their energy, it comes from the sun! This process is called photosynthesis, ______ helps plants grow strong. Some plants grow ______ flowers, while others grow fruits or vegetables. No matter ______ kind of plant it is, they all help make the world a greener place!

S: (Students begin reading the paragraph silently and circling the appropriate missing word.)

T: Now whisper-read your paragraph and see if you need to make any adjustments.

S: (Students whisper-read their paragraphs.)

T: Now read your paragraph to a partner. Take turns and make any corrections.

S: (Students take turns reading their paragraphs to their partners.)

T: Now let's read our paragraphs altogether. Make any adjustments.

TIPS

- You might provide a bank of function words and encourage students to select the best option for each sentence's semantic structure.
- This is loosely related to the beloved game of Mad Libs, so students might appreciate making a connection between this activity and that game. But instead of being silly, as students typically would be when playing Mad Libs, they should focus on accurate usage/application of words.

Step 4: Search & Stick

These are the menu options for Search & Stick, the step in the routine designed to help students automatically recognize the word. Our aim is immediate retrieval, efficiency, and connection to the word's use in text.

Word Part Chart It

Materials

- Piece of paper with three columns

WHAT: Manipulating word parts builds students' morphological awareness and broadens their word-analysis skills (Foorman et al., 2016). Here we lead students in breaking a word apart into its suffixes, prefixes, and roots so that they understand how they are applied and utilized in the formation of other words.

HOW: The script below serves to jumpstart your directions and conversation. The **T** is teacher-directed language, and the **S** indicates what students do.

T: We have been working on the word *disruption*. On your paper draw three columns. Write the three parts of the word across the three columns.

S: (Students create three columns, and write *dis-* at the top of one column, *rupt* in the middle column, and *-tion* in the last column.)

T: Underneath each word part write what it means.

S: (Students write meaning under each word part.)

T: Now write as many words that use this word part that you can think of in each column. Then compare with your neighbor and add words. For example:

- ***dis-***: *disobey, disorder, disrespect, disqualify, distract*
- ***rupt***: *disruptive, disrupt, erupt, corrupt, interrupt*
- ***-tion***: *declaration, deletion, projection, immigration, ignition*

S: (Students work independently, then in pairs.)

T: Now meet up with another group and add more words to your list.

S: (Students add more words.)

T: Now go back to your partner and take turns reading through the list of words. Look up the meaning for any words you don't know.

S: (Students take turns reading the three columns of words.)

TIP
Technology can be a great motivator for older students, so consider letting them use computers to search for words.

Build It

Materials

- Paper and pencil

WHAT: Explicitly teaching how words relate to one another not only develops students' vocabulary but also their spelling skills. This activity helps you do that. In addition, it has students read lists of words to improve their fluency.

HOW: The script below serves to jumpstart your directions and conversation. The **T** is teacher-directed language, and the **S** indicates what students do.

T: We have been working on the word *disruption*. We are going to come up with the words that are related to it. Choose one part of the word: the prefix, root, or suffix. Then write down as many words as possible that are related to that word part.

S: Students work with partners to generate lists of words that are related. For example:

- ***dis-***: *disruption, dismantle, disappear, disadvantage, disconnect, disagree*
- ***rupt***: *abrupt, rupture, interrupt, bankrupt, corrupt*
- ***-tion***: *ruption, action, absorption, education, acceleration, deflation*

> **T:** Now take turns reading through the lists of words you generated three times.
>
> **S:** (Students practice reading through their lists three times each.)
>
> **T:** Now trade lists with another partner group and read through their list.
>
> **S:** (Students practice reading through another group's list three times each.)
>
> **T:** Now trade lists with another partner group and read through their list.

TIPS

- Technology can be a great motivator for older students, so consider letting them use computers to search for words.
- If time permits, have students generate three word lists of words, one for each word part.

Hunt for It

Materials

- Text
- Small sticky notes
- Decodable and/or grade-level text

WHAT: It's not enough for students to recognize words in isolation; they must be able to transfer or extend what they've learned from our word-study instruction to connected text (Foorman et al., 2016). That's what this activity is designed to do.

HOW: The script below serves to jumpstart your directions and conversation. The **T** is teacher-directed language, and the **S** indicates what students do.

> **T:** We have been working with the word *disruption*. This word has the prefix *dis*- and suffix -*tion*. We are going to see if we can find those phonics patterns in other books that we read. When you read words that have either one of those prefixes or suffixes, place a sticky note next to it.
>
> **S:** (Students begin reading the book, and at the end of reading a section, they go back to place a sticky note on the page where they've located a word with a matching prefix or suffix.)

T: Nice job reading the book. Now flip through and remove all the sticky notes while you read each underlined word.

S: (Students read all the words as they remove the sticky notes.)

TIPS

- Begin by projecting a text passage and show students how to scan for the targeted linguistic feature—like the *-tion* example on page 128. Remind them that they are not looking solely for the exact word (like *disruption*) but rather words that either have the *-tion* suffix or the *dis-* prefix.
- For striving students, differentiate by narrowing the number of features for which students search. Above, they are looking for two patterns; some students might be better suited with just the prefix or suffix.
- If your students might benefit from another writing opportunity, have them transcribe the words in their notebooks.

In Closing, Remember...

Full speed ahead to fluency! As our full-alphabetic and consolidated alphabetic phase students increase their efficiency with multisyllabic words, they begin to explore how morphology and how origins of words influence their spellings and meanings. The Making Words Stick Menu for grades 4 and 5 helps students map longer words in their minds, which give them more mental energy to comprehend and enjoy texts.

CONCLUSION

We started the book with the fascinating fact that the average adult reader has knowledge of about 50,000 words that he or she instantly and effortlessly recognizes (Mather & Jaffe, 2021). Our aim in this book was to explain the brain processes that enable the mapping of words, the research and theories underpinning the process, and why instant recognition of words matters in students' literacy development.

Our intent in writing this book was to translate the enormously important research on orthographic mapping and make it both comprehensible and applicable to teachers. We wrote it because of our conviction that the high-quality research found behind academic paywalls and in peer-reviewed journals belongs in the hands of those who need it most—educators. Writing this book felt like a gift to our previous selves as early career teachers, and to the students in our classrooms: Molly attempting to teach spelling in her 1999 classroom in Oakland, and Katie aiming to increase her kindergartners' high-frequency word identification in her Colorado classroom. And let's not forget that as reading researchers, we are fascinated with the neuroscience of the reading circuitry; had we better understood it as classroom teachers, our classroom instruction might have looked vastly different.

Here are the big takeaways that we hope you carry into your classroom:

- The miracle of reading is made possible by a series of neural connections between multiple areas of the brain, and these connections are facilitated by direct, explicit instruction.
- Orthographic mapping is the cognitive process of learning to read words by sight and spell them from memory. It is essential for fluent reading and comprehension. To map words, we must connect the spelling of a word to its pronunciation and meaning. The trifecta of how a word

looks, how it sounds, and what it means facilitates a reader's ability to store and retrieve that word.

- An understanding of Linnea Ehri's phases of word reading and spelling development allows us to know what students need and when to provide that targeted, explicit instruction.
- Memorizing words is simply not a possible nor sustainable route to fluent reading. Similarly, relying on visual memory as a spelling strategy is ineffective; Joshi and colleagues (2008) wrote, "Many assumptions about the nature of spelling—including the widespread belief that it is visual-memory skill—are misinformed."

Armed with an instructional routine that's grounded in both theory and research, you'll make words stick for readers and allow them to cruise with clear skies and no turbulence into lifelong literacy.

Appendix

Download all the items in this appendix.

Appendix	Title
A	Lesson Planning Sheets
B	Count and Box Letters
C	Word Part Organizer
D	Word Blending
E	Count and Box Syllables
F	Word Web
G	Word Expert Card
H	Word Ladder
I	Look-Alike Word Activity
J	Root Word Tree
K	Frayer Model

Lesson Planning Sheet

Word(s): ____________________

Steps From the Routine	Activities From the Menu	Page Numbers
See & Say		
Segment & Spell		
Study & Suss Out		
Search & Stick		

Lesson Planning Sheet

Word(s): ____________________

Steps From the Routine	Activities From the Menu	Page Numbers
See & Say		
Segment & Spell		
Study & Suss Out		
Search & Stick		

Count and Box Letters

Word Part Organizer

Target Word + Ending =

Target Word + Ending =

Target Word + Ending =

Target Word + Ending =

Word Blending

Count and Box Syllables

Word Web

Definition #1
Synonym
Antonym
Target Word
Example
Category
Definition #2

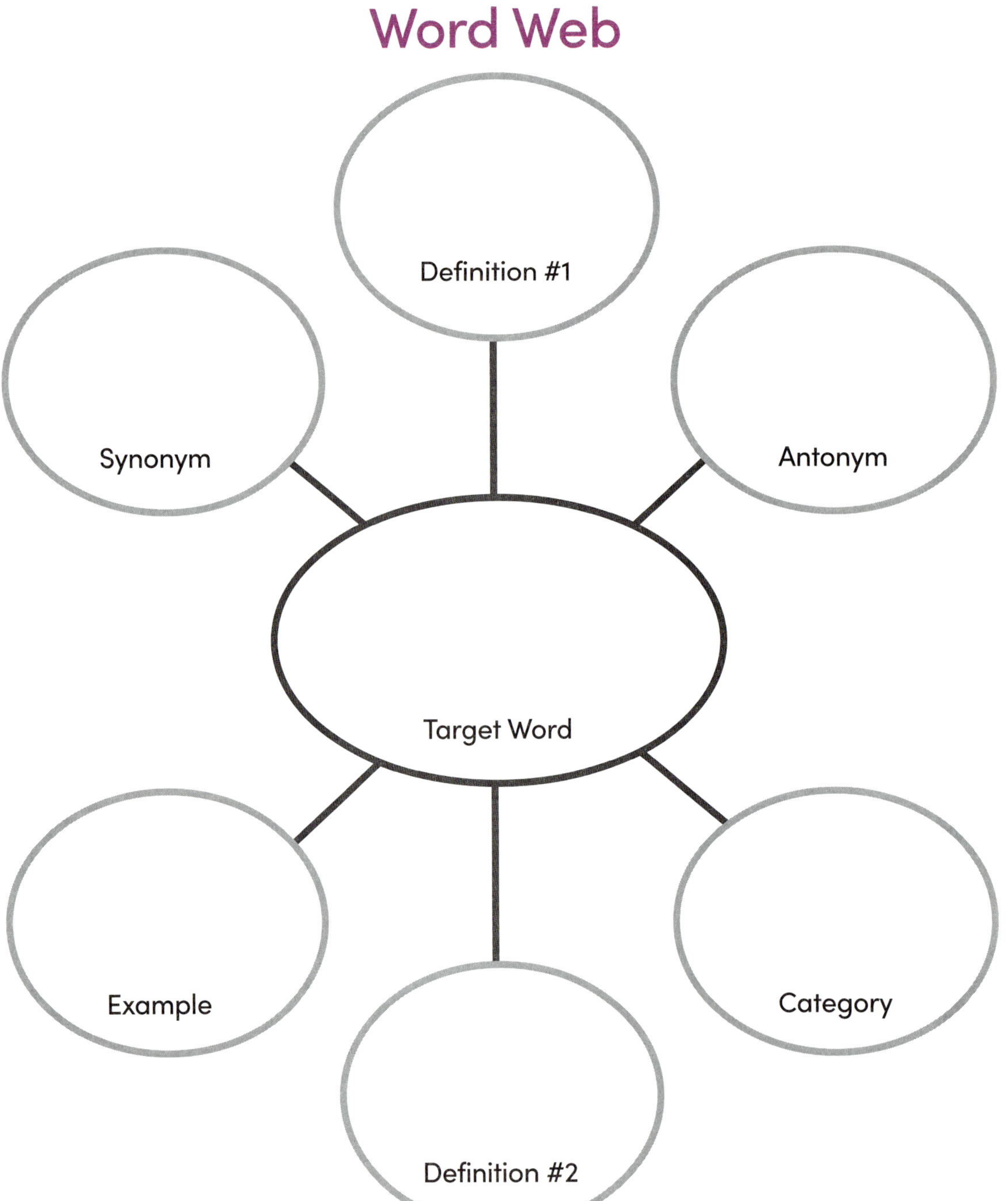

Word Expert Card

Name: ______________________________

Word	**My definition**
A picture of the word	**A sentence using the word**

Word Ladder

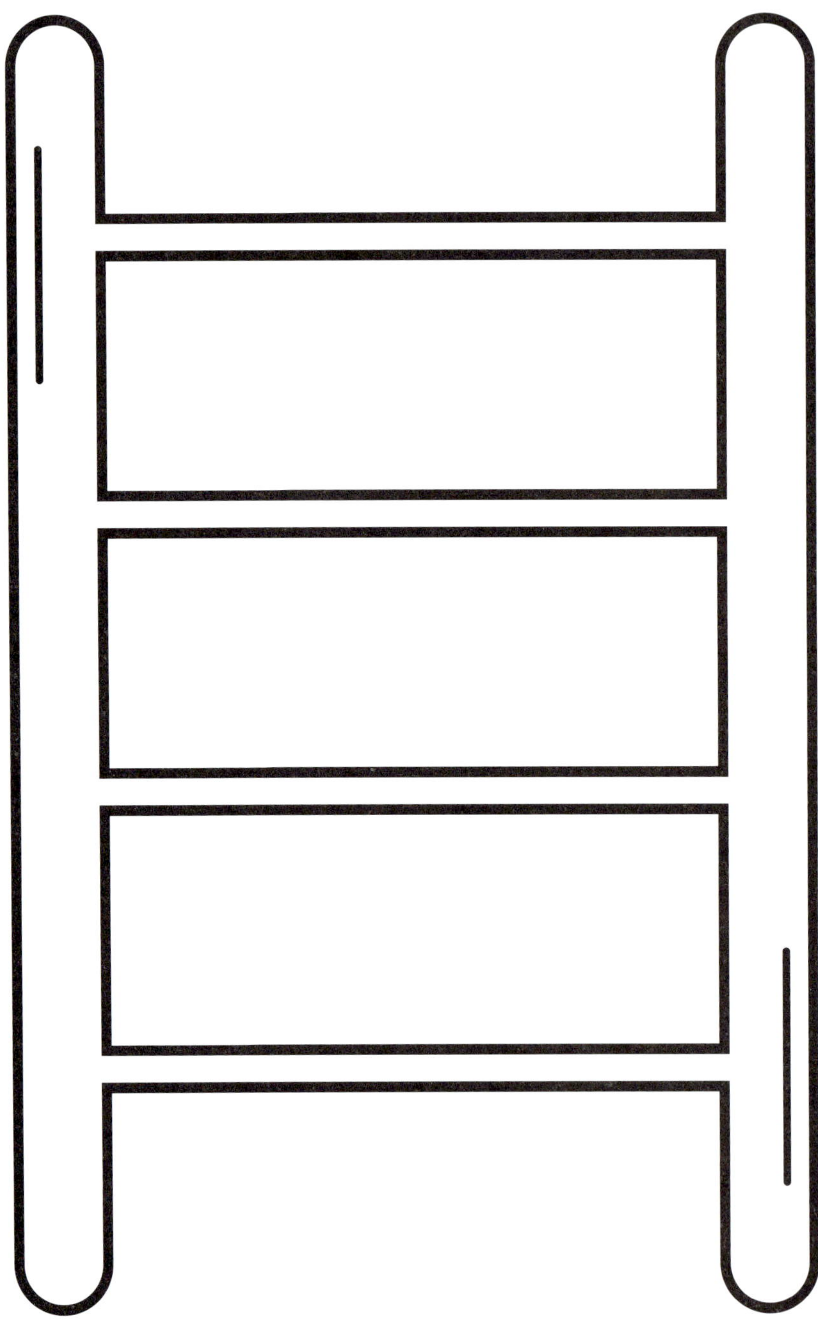

Look-Alike Word Activity

Root Word Tree

Root: ______________________________

Meaning: ______________________________

Origin: ______________________________

Roots are word parts that have meaning.

Frayer Model

Name: ______________________________

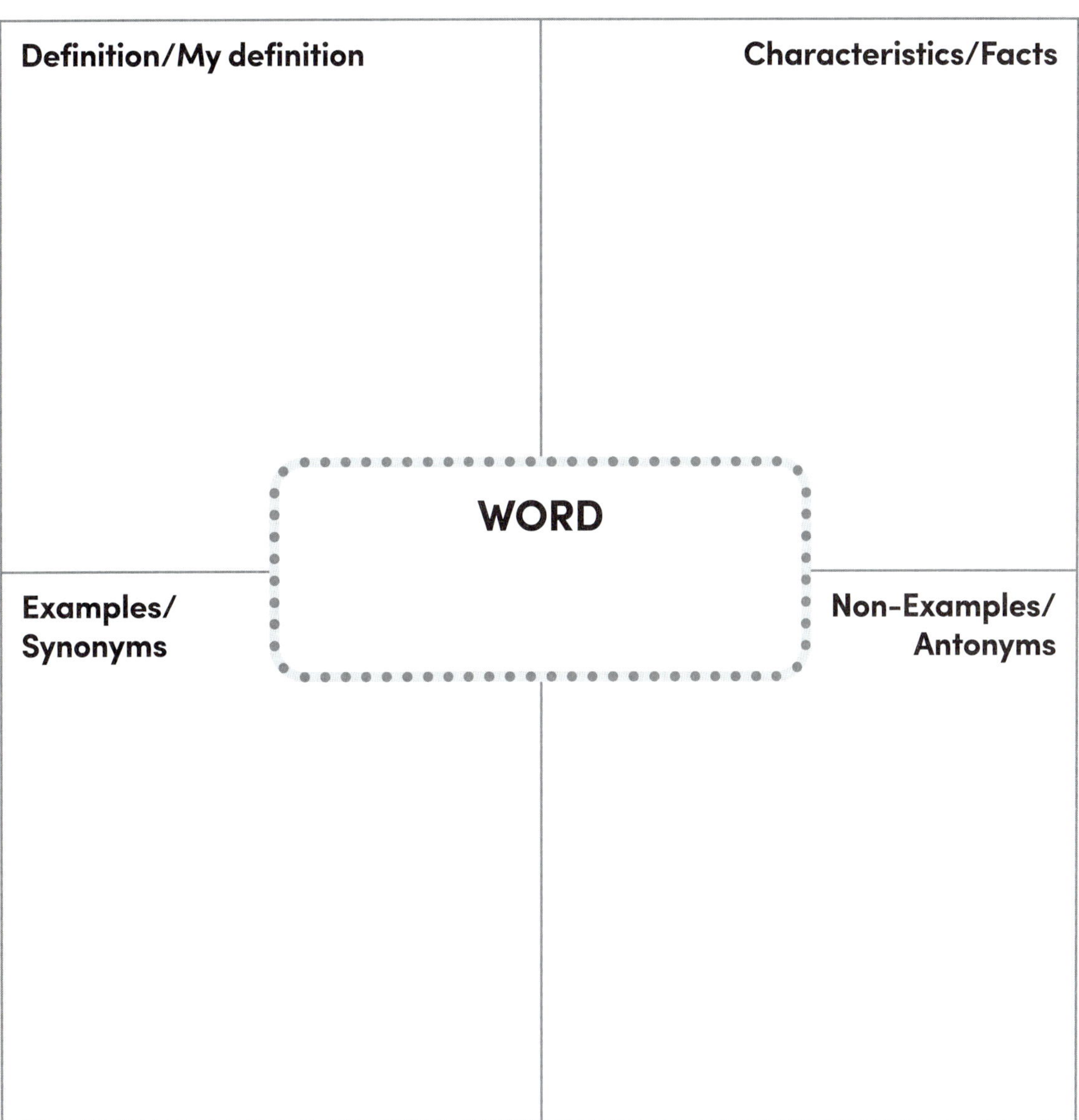

REFERENCES

Aaron, P., Wilczynski, S., & Keetay, S. (1998). The anatomy of word-specific memory in C. Hulme & R. M. Joshi (Eds). *Reading and spelling: Development and disorders*. Routledge. 405–419.

Anderson, R. C., Hiebert, E. H., Scott, J. A., & Wilkinson, I. A. G. (1985). *Becoming a nation of readers: The report of the commission on reading*. National Academy of Education.

Archer, A. L., Gleason, M. M., & Vachon, V. L. (2003). Decoding and fluency: Foundation skills for struggling older readers. *Learning Disability Quarterly, 26*(2), 89–101.

Barnes, E. M., Hadley, E. B., Lawson-Adams, J., & Dickinson, D. K. (2023). Nonverbal supports for word learning: Prekindergarten teachers' gesturing practices during shared book reading. *Early Childhood Research Quarterly, 64*, 302–312.

Baumann, J. F., Edwards, E. C., Boland, E., Olejnik, S., & Kame'enui, E. (2003). Vocabulary tricks: Effects of instruction in morphology and context on fifth grade students' ability to derive and infer word meanings. *American Educational Research Journal, 40*(2), 447–494.

Bear, D. R., Invernizzi, M. A., Templeton, W. S., & Johnston, F. (2020). *Words their way: Phonics, vocabulary, and spelling instruction* (7th ed.). Allyn & Bacon.

Beck, I., McKeown, M., & Kucan, L. (2013). *Bringing words to life: Robust vocabulary instruction*. The Guilford Press.

Booton, S., Wonnacott, E., Hodgkiss, A., Mathers, S., & Murphy, V. (2022). Children's knowledge of multiple word meanings: Which factors count and for whom? *Applied Linguistics, 43*(2), 293–315.

Bowers, P., Kirby, J., & Deacon, S. (2010). The effects of morphological instruction on literacy skills: A systematic review of the literature. *Review of Educational Research, 80*(2), 144–179.

Brady, S. (2020). A 2020 perspective on research findings on alphabetics (phoneme awareness and phonics): Implications for instruction. *The Reading League Journal, 1*(3), 20–28.

Bransford, J. D., Brown, A. L., & Cocking, R. R. (Eds.). (1999). *How people learn: Brain, mind, experience, and school*. National Academy Press.

Cassar, M., Treiman, R., Moats, L., Pollo, T., & Kessler, B. (2005). How do the spellings of children with dyslexia compare with those of nondyslexic children? *Reading and Writing, 18*, 27–49.

Chambré, S. J., Ehri, L. C., & Ness, M. (2017). Orthographic facilitation of first graders' vocabulary learning: Does directing attention to print enhance the effect. *Reading and Writing, 30*(5), 1137–1156.

Colenbrander, D., Kohnen, S., Beyersmann, E., Robidoux, S., Wegener, S., Arrow, T., ... Castles, A. (2022). Teaching children to read irregular words: A comparison of three instructional methods. *Scientific Studies of Reading, 26*(6), 545–564.

Colenbrander, D., Miles, K. P., & Ricketts, J. (2019). To see or not to see: How does seeing spellings support vocabulary learning? *Language, Speech, and Hearing Services in Schools, 50*(4), 609–628.

Dahaene, S. (2009). *Reading in the brain*. Viking.

Dehaene, S. (2013). *Inside the Letterbox: How literacy transforms the human brain*. Cerebrum.

Dolch, E. W. (1936). A basic sight vocabulary. *The Elementary School Journal, 36*(6), 456–460.

Ehri, L. C. (1992). Reconceptualizing the development of sight word reading and its relationship to recoding. In P. B. Gough, L. C. Ehri, & R. Treiman (Eds.), *Reading acquisition* (pp. 107–143). Lawrence Erlbaum Associates.

Ehri, L. C. (1998). Grapheme-phoneme knowledge is essential to learning to read words in English. In J. L. Metsala & L. C. Ehri (Eds.), *Word recognition in beginning literacy* (pp. 3–40). Lawrence Erlbaum Associates.

Ehri, L. C. (2000). Learning to read and learning to spell: Two sides of a coin. *Topics in Language Disorders, 20*(3), 19–36.

Ehri, L. C. (2005). Development of sight word reading: Phases and findings. In M. J. Snowling & C. Hulme (Eds.), *The science of reading: A handbook* (pp. 135–154). Blackwell Publishing.

Ehri, L. C. (2014). Orthographic mapping in the acquisition of sight word reading, spelling memory, and vocabulary learning. *Scientific Studies of Reading, 18*, 5–21.

Ehri, L. C. (2020). The science of learning to read words: A case for systematic phonics instruction. *Reading Research Quarterly, 55*(S1), S45–S60.

Ehri, L. C. (2022). What teachers need to know and do to teach letter-sounds, phonemic awareness, word reading, and phonics. *The Reading Teacher, 76*(1), 53–61.

Ehri, L. C. (2023). Phases of development in learning to read and spell words. *American Educator*, 17–18.

Ehri, L. C., & Saltmarsh, J. (1995). Beginning readers outperform older disabled readers in learning to read words by sight. *Reading and Writing: An Interdisciplinary Journal, 7*(3), 295–326.

Ehri, L. C., & Wilce, L. (1985). Movement into reading: Is the first stage of printed word learning visual or phonetic? *Reading Research Quarterly, 20*(2), 163–179.

Elkonin, D. B. (1973). U.S.S.R. In J. Downing (Ed.), *Comparative reading: Cross-national studies of behavior and processes in reading and writing* (pp. 551–579). Macmillan.

Foorman, B., Beyler, N., Borradaile, K., Coyne, M., Denton, C. A., Dimino, J., Furgeson, J., Hayes, L., Henke, J., Justice, L., Keating, B., Lewis, W., Sattar, S., Streke, A., Wagner, R., & Wissel, S. (2016). *Foundational skills to support reading for understanding in kindergarten through 3rd grade* (NCEE 2016-4008). National Center for Education Evaluation and Regional Assistance (NCEE).

Frayer, D., Frederick, W. C., & Klausmeier, H. J. (1969). *A schema for testing the level of cognitive mastery.* Wisconsin Center for Education Research.

Gentry, J. R. (2004). *The science of spelling: The explicit specifics that make great readers and writers* (1st ed.). Heinemann.

Gentry, J. R., & Ouellette, G. (2025). *Brain words: How the science of reading informs teaching*. Stenhouse.

Gonzalez-Frey, S. M., & Ehri, L. C. (2021). Connected phonation is more effective than segmented phonation for teaching beginning readers to decode unfamiliar words. *Scientific Studies of Reading, 25*(3), 272–285.

Goodwin, A. P., & Ahn, S. (2013). A meta-analysis of morphological interventions in English: Effects on literacy outcomes for school-age children. *Scientific Studies of Reading, 17*(4), 257–285.

Graham, S., Harris, K. R., & Chorzempa, B. F. (2002). Contribution of spelling instruction to the spelling, writing, and reading of poor spellers. *Journal of Educational Psychology, 94*(4), 669–686.

Graham, S., & Santangelo, T. (2014). Does spelling instruction make students better spellers, readers, and writers? A meta-analytic review. *Reading and Writing, 27*(9), 1703–1743.

Green, K., Keogh, K., & Prout, J. (2024). The CPB sight words: A new research-based high-frequency word list for early reading instruction. *The Reading Teacher, 78*(1), 56–64.

Hadley, E., Dickinson, D., Hirsh-Pasek, K., & Golinkoff, R. (2018). Building semantic networks: The impact of a vocabulary intervention on preschoolers' depth of word knowledge. *Reading Research Quarterly, 54*(1), 41–61.

Harris, A., & Jacobsen, M. (1973-1974). Some comparisons between 'basic elementary reading vocabularies' and other word lists. *Reading Research Quarterly, 9*(1), 87–109.

Honig, B., Beard, El-Dinary, P., Hudson, R. F., Lane, H. B., Mahler, J., & Pullen, P. C. (2018). *Teaching reading sourcebook* (3rd ed.). Arena Press.

Joseph, L. M. (2000). Developing first graders' phonemic awareness, word identification, and spelling: A comparison of two contemporary phonic instructional approaches. *Literacy Research and Instruction, 39*(2), 161–190.

Joshi, R., Treiman, R., Carreker, S., & Moats, L. (2008). How words cast their spell spelling is an integral part of learning the language, not a matter of memorization. *American Educator.*

Just, M. A., & Carpenter, P. A. (1987). *The psychology of reading and language comprehension*. Allyn and Bacon.

Kamil, M. L., Borman, G. D., Dole, J., Kral, C. C., Salinger, T., and Torgesen, J. (2008). *Improving adolescent literacy: Effective classroom and intervention practices: A practice guide.* National Center for Education Evaluation and Regional Assistance.

Kearns, D. M., & Borkenhagen, M. (2024). Following the rules in an unruly writing system: The cognitive science of learning to read English. *The Reading Teacher, 77*(5), 712–726.

Kearns, D. M., Steacy, L. M., Compton, D. L., Gilbert, J. K., Goodwin, A., Cho, E., Lindstrom, E. R., & Collins, A. A. (2016). Modeling polymorphemic word recognition: Exploring differences among children with early-emerging and late-emerging word reading difficulty. *Journal of Learning Disabilities, 49*(4), 368–394.

Kearns, D. M., & Whaley, V. (2019). Helping students with dyslexia read long words using syllables and morphemes. *Teaching Exceptional Children, 51*(3), 212–225.

Keesey, S., Konrad, M., & Joseph, L. M. (2015). Word boxes improve phonemic awareness, letter-sound correspondences, and spelling skills of at-risk kindergartners. *Remedial and Special Education, 36*(3).

Kemeny, L. (2023). *7 Mighty moves: Research-backed classroom-tested strategies to ensure K–3 reading success.* Scholastic.

Kilpatrick, D. (2015). *Essentials of assessing, preventing, and overcoming reading difficulties*. John Wiley & Sons.

Kim, Y., & Petscher, Y. (2023). Do spelling and vocabulary improve classification accuracy of children's reading difficulties over and above word reading? *Reading Research Quarterly, 58*(2), 240–253.

Kim, Y., Wolters, A., & Lee, J. (2024). Reading and writing relations are not uniform. They differ by the linguistic grain size, developmental phase, and measurement. *Review of Educational Research, 94*(3), 311–342.

Lansdown, S. (1991). Increasing vocabulary knowledge using direct instruction, cooperative grouping, and reading in junior high school. *Illinois Reading Council Journal, 9*(4), 15–21.

Lilienfeld, S., Lynn, S., & Namy, L. (2018). *Psychology: From inquiry to understanding*. Pearson.

Loftus, M., & Sappington, L. (2024). *The literacy 50: Real-world answers to questions about reading that keep you up at night*. Scholastic.

Mather, N., & Jaffe, L. (2021). Orthographic knowledge is essential for reading and spelling. *The Reading League Journal*, 15–21.

Mesmer, H. (2024). *Big words for young readers: Teaching kids in grades K to 5 to decode—and understand—words with multiple syllables and morphemes*. Scholastic.

Miles, K. P., & Ehri, L. C. (2017). Learning to read words on flashcards: Effects of sentence contexts and word class in native and nonnative English-speaking kindergartners. *Early Childhood Research Quarterly, 41*, 103–113.

Miles, K. P., & Ehri, L. (2019). Orthographic mapping facilitates sight word memory and vocabulary learning. In D. A. Kilpatrick, R. Malatesha Joshi, & R. K. Wagner (Eds.), *Reading development and difficulties.*

Miles, K. P., Eide, D., & Butler, J. (2024). The regularity of high-frequency words (sight words): Teacher phonetic knowledge is key. *Reading Psychology.*

Miles, K. P., McFadden, A., & Ehri, L. (2018). Associations between language and literacy skills and sight word learning for native and nonnative English-speaking kindergarteners. *Reading and Writing, 32*(7).

Miles, K. P., Rubin, G., & Gonzalez-Frey, S. (2017). Rethinking sight words. *The Reading Teacher, 71*(6), 715–726.

Moats, L. C., & Farrell, M. L. (2005). Multisensory structured language education. In J. R. Birsh (Ed.), *Multisensory teaching of basic language skills*, (pp. 23–41). Paul Brookes Publishing.

Murray, B., McIlwain, M., Wang, G., & Finley, S. (2019). How do beginners learn to read irregular words as sight words? *Journal of Research in Reading, 42*(1), 123–146.

Pan, S., Rickard, T., & Bjork, R. (2021). Does spelling still matter—and if so, how should it be taught? Perspectives from contemporary and historical research. *Educational Psychology Review, 33*, 1523–1552.

Perfetti, C. (2007). Reading ability: Lexical quality to comprehension. *Scientific Studies of Reading, 11*(4), 357–383.

Peters, C. (1974). A comparison between the Frayer Model of concept attainment and the textbook approach to concept attainment. *Reading Research Quarterly, Vol. 10*(4), 651–663.

Phillips, B. M., Clancy-Menchetti, J., & Lonigan, C. J. (2008). Successful phonological awareness instruction with preschool children: Lessons from the classroom. *Topics in Early Childhood Special Education, 28*(1), 3–17.

Pullen, P., & Lane, H. (2016). Hands-on decoding: Guidelines for using manipulative letters. *Learning Disabilities: A Multidisciplinary Journal, 21*(1), 27–37.

Putnam, R. (2017). Using research to make informed decisions about the spelling curriculum. *Texas Journal of Literacy Education, 5*(1), 24–32.

Rashotte, C. A., MacPhee, K., & Torgesen, J. K. (2001). The effectiveness of a group reading instruction program with poor readers in multiple grades. *Learning Disability Quarterly, 24*(2), 119–134.

Reitsma, P. (1983). Printed word learning in beginning readers. *Journal of Experimental Child Psychology, 36*, 321–339.

Report of the National Reading Panel. (2000). *Teaching children to read: Reports of the subgroups*. Eunice Kennedy Shriver National Institute of Child Health and Human Development, NIH, DHHS.

Richek, M. (2005). Words are wonderful: Interactive, time-efficient strategies to teach meaning vocabulary. *The Reading Teacher, 58*(5), 414–423.

Ricketts, J., Bishop, D. V. M., & Nation, K. (2009). Orthographic facilitation in oral vocabulary acquisition. *The Quarterly Journal of Experimental Psychology, 62*(10), 1948–1966.

Rosenthal, J., & Ehri, L. C. (2008). The mnemonic value of orthography for vocabulary learning. *Journal of Educational Psychology, 100*(1), 175–191.

Rosenthal, J., & Ehri, L. C. (2011). Pronouncing new words aloud during the silent reading of text enhances fifth graders' memory for vocabulary words and their spellings. *Reading and Writing: An Interdisciplinary Journal, 24*(8), 921–950.

Ross, K., & Joseph, L. (2019). Effects of word boxes on improving students' basic literacy skills: A literature review. *Preventing School Failure, 63*(1), 43–51.

Seidenberg, M. S., & McClelland, J. L. (1989). A distributed, developmental model of word recognition and naming. *Psychological Review, 96*(4), 523–568.

Seymour, T., Pittman, R., Binks-Cantrell, E., & Joshi, M. (2024). The case for the inclusion of spelling in early literacy assessments. *The Reading League Journal.*

Shanahan, T. (2022, June 11). Explicit spelling instruction or invented spelling? *Shanahan on Literacy*. www.shanahanonliteracy.com/blog/explicit-spelling-instruction-or-invented-spelling

Share, D. L. (1999). Phonological recoding and orthographic learning: A direct test of the self-teaching hypothesis. *Journal of Experimental Child Psychology, 72*(2), 95–129.

Share, D. L. (2011). On the role of phonology in reading acquisition: The self-teaching hypothesis. In S. A. Brady, D. Braze, & C. A. Fowler (Eds.), *Explaining individual differences in reading: Theory and evidence* (pp. 45–68). Psychology Press.

Share, D. L. (2011). Orthographic learning, phonological recording, and self-teaching. *Advances in Child Development and Behavior, 36*, 31–82.

Simonsen, F., & Gunter, L. (2001). Best practices in spelling instruction: A research summary. *Journal of Direct Instruction, 1*(2), 97–105.

Steacy, L., Wade-Woolley, L., Rueckl, J., Pugh, K., Elliot, J., & Compton, D. (2020). The role of set for variability in irregular word reading: Word and child predictors in typically developing readers and students at-risk for reading disabilities. *Scientific Studies of Reading, 23*(6), 523–532.

Stuart, M., Masterson, J., & Dixon, M. (2000). Spongelike acquisition of sight vocabulary in beginning readers? *Journal of Research in Reading, 23*(1), 12–27.

Vaughn, S., Gersten, R., Dimino, J., Taylor, M. J., Newman-Gonchar, R., Krowka, S., Kieffer, M. J., McKeown, M., Reed, D., Sanchez, M., St. Martin, K., Wexler, J., Morgan, S., Yañez, A., & Jayanthi, M. (2022). *Providing reading interventions for students in grades 4–9* (WWC 2022007). U.S. Department of Education.

Wang, Z., O'Reilly, T., & Sutherland, R. (2024). *Replicating decoding threshold in ReadBasix®: Impact on reading skills development* (Research Memorandum No. RM-24-06). ETS.

Wasowicz, J. (2021). A speech-to-print approach to teaching reading. *LDA Bulletin, 53*(2), 9–18.

Winters, R. (2009). Interactive frames for vocabulary growth and word consciousness. *The Reading Teacher, 62*(8), 685–690.

Wolf, M. (2008). *Proust and the squid: The story and science of the reading brain*. Harper Perennial.

INDEX

A

accuracy, 41, 45, 82, 115, 118
activities, about, 46–47
  choosing words for, 48–49
  for grades K and 1, 55–57
  for grades 2 and 3, 88–90
  for grades 4 and 5, 120–122
affixes, 25, 27
  activities with, 104–105, 123, 124, 128–129, 136–137, 137–138, 138–139
  in benchmarks, 87, 119
  consolidated alphabetic reader and, 117
  full-alphabetic reader and, 85
alliteration, 14
alphabet knowledge, in scope and sequence, 48, 57
alphabetic principle, pre-alphabetic readers and, 51
analogy, as reading strategy, 22
angular gyrus, 20, 28
antonyms, 99–100, 130–131
articulation, activity with, 60–61
assessments of spelling, 119
"auditory bombardment," 42, 49
automaticity, 41, 45

B

base words. *See* roots
benchmarks, by grade, 53, 87, 119
blending, 17, 24, 41, 85, 112
  in benchmark, 53, 87
  in activity, 91
"bossy *e*"/VC*e* rule, 85
brain processes, 7–8, 12, 15–28, 39, 42–43, 140
brain regions, 13–14, 19–21, 59
Broca's Area, 20–21, 27

C

categories of words, 29–33
  by decodability, 34–37
cerebellum, 20
characteristics of words, 81, 100, 130–131, 153
Children's Picture Book (CPB) sight words, 31
chunking, activities with, 123, 124, 125
cognitive energy, 19, 20, 26, 118
compound words, 48, 53, 75–76
connected text, activities with, 83, 112–113, 138–139
consolidated alphabetic readers, 25, 34, 117–118
consonant digraphs, in scope and sequence, 48, 57
consonant blends, 27, 48, 53, 57
consonant clusters, activity with, 112
consonants, in scope and sequence, 48, 57
context clues, in reading, 22
context, words used in, activities with, 43–44, 45, 101–102, 105–106
Count and Box Letters (Appendix B), 144
  activities with, 64–65, 95–96
Count and Box Syllables (Appendix E), 147
  activity with, 126–127
cursive, 42, 94
CVC words, 34, 53, 56

D

decodable texts, 32–33, 38, 83, 112, 138–139
decoding, 9, 14, 18, 22, 26, 41, 50, 120
  activities for, 45, 65–66, 106–107
"decoding threshold," 120
definitions, activities using, 99–100, 101–102, 105–106, 130–131
dictionaries, 11, 16, 44
  activity with, 128–129
digraphs, 27, 53, 54, 85
diphthongs, in scope and sequence, grades 2 and 3, 90
Dolch List, 11, 30, 33, 34, 38
drawing, activity with, 69–70
dry-erase boards, activities using, 63, 67

E

Elkonin Boxes, 116
  activities using, 64–65, 95–96
encoding, 18, 41, 50
  activities for, 45, 65–66, 68
endings, 45, 85, 145
  in scope and sequence, 90
  activities with, 74–76, 104–105, 113–114
English, 44 phonemes in, 17, 85
etymology, 49, 50
explicit instruction, 40, 49, 50, 116, 119

F

final *e*, in scope and sequence, grades K and 1, 57
finger sliding, in activity, 91
flash words, 30
flash card drills, ineffective, 37
fluency, 27, 41, 45
fly swatter, activity with, 82
fonts, activities with, 42, 94
Frayer Model (Appendix K), 153

activity with, 130–131
frontal lobe, 20–21, 27, 42
Fry List, 30, 38
full-alphabetic readers, 24–25, 27, 34, 85–86
function words, 27, 29, 33, 38
activities with, 77–80, 108–111, 132–135

G

grammatical relationships, activities with, 77–78, 108–109, 132–133
grapheme-phoneme conversion, in brain, 20–21, 28
grapheme-phoneme correspondence, 23, 25, 41, 52–53
activities with, 43, 63, 64–65, 95–96, 126–127
Greek words, 50, 117, 122

H

handwriting, activities with, 42, 96–97
Heart Words, 30
high-frequency words, 16, 29–37, 38, 49, 140
in benchmarks, 87, 119
drilling with cards, 11–12, 37

I

instructional routine, 13, 39–40
choosing words for, 48–49
grades K and 1, 55–84
grades 2 and 3, 88–89
grades 4 and 5, 120–139
menu of activities in, 46–47
overview, 39–45
research that informs, 41
irregularly spelled words, 29–30, 33, 34–37, 97
in benchmarks, 87, 116

K

kinesthetics, in activities, 62, 67, 70, 71

L

Latin words, 117, 129
Lesson Planning Sheets (Appendix A), 143
use of, to select activities, 56, 89, 121
letter knowledge, 51–53
letters, activities with, 42, 65–66, 68, 94, 96–97, 97–98, 114–115
letter-sound correspondence, 14, 17, 23, 24, 27, 38, 48–49, 84, 86
activities with, 64–65, 126–127
partial-alphabetic readers and, 52–53
linguistic backgrounds, diversity of, 39–40
linguistic features of words, 36, 45, 49, 139
literacy development, 7, 14, 18, 40, 140
long vowels, 48, 53, 57, 89, 90
activity for, 57, 63
Look-Alike Word Activity (Appendix I), 151
activity with, 114–115
lowercase, 42, 53

M

Mad Libs-like activity, for function words, 80, 111, 135
magnetic letters, activities using, 46, 65–66, 68
magnifying glass, activities using, 83, 112, 138–139
manipulatives, 68, 95–96, 126–127
markers, activities using, 63, 67, 69–70
meaning, 13, 23, 25, 140
activities for, 43–44, 74–76
in brain, 20–21
medial vowel sounds, 34, 38
memorization, rote, ineffective, 8, 12, 21, 29, 33, 37, 141
menus of activities, 46–49
grades K and 1, 55
grades 2 and 3, 88
grades 4 and 5, 120
mirrors, in activities, 60–61, 93
morphemes, 41, 118
activities with, 74–76, 81, 124, 128–129
morphology, 14, 27, 117, 119
activities with, 43–44, 136–137, 104–105
mouth formations, activities with, 60–61, 93
multilingual learners, 33, 69–70, 101
multiple meanings, activities with, 73, 99–100, 102–103, 105–106
multisyllabic words, 41, 86, 117, 119
activities with, 62, 123, 124, 125, 126–127, 128–129, 130–131

N

Need-to-Know Words, 30
neural networks, 13, 14, 19, 21, 140
neurodivergence, 39–40, 69–70

O

occipital lobe, 20, 28, 42
onset-rime, 14, 43, 50
orthographic mapping, 9–10, 13, 14, 140–141
benchmarks for, 53, 87, 119
mechanics of, 16–21
skills for, 23
orthographic representation, activities with, 42, 94

P

partial-alphabetic readers, 24–25, 27, 34, 52–53, 84
period, activities with, 77–78, 108–109, 132–133
permanently irregularly spelled, 34–37
phases of reading development, 24–25
phonemes, 44 in English, 17, 85
phonemic awareness, 14, 23, 84
activities with, 43, 64–65, 65–66, 67, 91, 106–107
phonetic concepts, 12, 48–49, 119
phonics knowledge, in benchmarks, 87, 119
phonics patterns, activities with, 112–113, 138–139
phonological awareness, 13, 40, 51–52
activities with, 42, 63, 92
Popcorn Words, 30
Power Words, 30
pre-alphabetic readers, 24–25, 27, 34, 51–52, 84, 117
prediction, as reading strategy, 22
prefixes, 25, 121
in benchmarks, 87, 119
consolidated alphabetic reader and, 117
full-alphabetic reader and, 85
activities with, 104–105, 123, 124, 128–129, 136–137, 137–138, 138–139
print, 14, 17, 23, 50, 94
pronunciation, 27, 55, 140
activities with, 42, 60–61, 93, 97–98, 113–114
in benchmarks, 119
in orthographic mapping, 17, 22

in phases of reading development, 25
proper nouns, decoding, 9
punctuation, activities with, 77–78, 108–109, 132–133

Q

question mark, activities with, 77–78, 108–109, 132–133

R

r-controlled vowels, 54, 85, 89, 90
reading circuitry, 19, 21, 28, 59
reading development, phases of (Ehri's), 21, 24–25, 27, 34, 51–53, 85–86, 117–118, 141
reading strategies, typical, 22–23
reading vs. spelling, 18, 54, 86–87, 119
Ready4Reading program, Scholastic's, 48
regularly spelled words, 29, 34–35, 38, 97
in benchmarks, 87, 119
research behind instructional routine, 41
rhyming, 14, 16, 101
Root Word Tree (Appendix J), 152
activity with, 128–129
roots, 25, 27, 47, 117
activities with, 122, 123, 124, 128–129, 136–137, 137–138, 138–139
in benchmarks, 87, 119

S

scope and sequence, 10, 14, 32, 34–35, 53, 56, 87
recommended, 57, 90, 122
Scholastic's Ready4Reading program, 48
segmenting, 17, 24, 41, 55, 88, 121
activities with, 43, 63, 67
in benchmarks, 53, 87
partial-alphabetic readers and, 52–53
self-correcting, 125
semantic features, activity with, 43–44
semantics, 28, 50
semantics, in brain, 20–21, 28
short vowels, 48, 57, 61, 114
sight words, 30–33
in benchmarks, 119
silent letters, 36–37
silent reading, in activities, 79, 110, 134–135
Snap Words, 30
sound boxes, activities with, 64–65, 95–96
sound wall, 60–61
"sounding out" words, 14, 91
special spellings, in scope and sequence, 48
speech language pathologist, 60, 61
activities with, 63, 65–66, 106–107, 114–115, 137–138
spelling, 25, 27, 41, 54, 55, 88
spelling patterns, activities with, 81, 95–96, 113–114
spelling rules, full-alphabetic reader and, 85–86
spelling tests, 10–11
spelling vs. reading, 18, 54, 86–87, 119
spinal cord, 20
sticky notes, activities using, 83, 112, 138–139
stopwatches, 46
suffixes, 25, 85, 117
activities with, 104–105, 123, 124, 128–129, 136–137, 137–138, 138–139
in benchmarks, 87, 119
sussing out (term), 44
swatch cards, activity with, 102–103
syllables, 14, 25, 27
activities with, 43, 62, 92, 93, 125, 126–127, 128–129
synonyms, activities with, 99–100, 130–131
syntax, in brain, 20–21, 28

T

temporal lobe, 20–21, 28, 42
temporarily irregularly spelled words, 34–35, 36, 38
thesaurus, use of, 103

U

underlining, activities with, 83, 97–98, 112–113, 124, 138–139
uppercase, 42, 53

V

VCe rule, 53, 54, 85
visual cues, 24, 51
visual processing, 20, 28, 42
visual representations, activities with, 69–70, 71
vocabulary, activities with, 73, 102–103, 106–107, 137–138
vocalizing, 59
vowel sounds, activities with, 61, 62, 113–114, 123
vowel teams, 27, 54, 85, 89
vowels, complex, in scope and sequence, 48, 90

W

Wernicke's Area, 20–21, 28
whisper reading, activities with, 79–80, 111, 134–135
word analysis, 16, 23, 48–49, 88
activities with, 74–76, 136–137
word banks, function, 79, 110, 134
Word Blending (Appendix D), 146
activity with, 91
word cards, 11–12
activities with, 77–78, 108–109, 132–133
Word Expert Card (Appendix G), 149
activity with, 101–102
"word hunts," 10, 45
activities with, 83–84, 112–113, 138–139
Word Ladder (Appendix H), 150
activity with, 106–107
word lists, 30
Word Part Organizer (Appendix C), 145
activities with, 74–76, 104–105
word recognition, 19, 41, 45, 118
word study, 49
activities with, 83, 112–113, 138–139
in scope and sequence, 48
Word Web (Appendix F), 148
activity with, 99–100
words, categories of, 29–33
by decodability, 34–37
Word-Wall Words, 30
writing, 41, 48–49, 119, 139
activities with, 64–65, 73, 94, 96–97, 99–100, 106, 125
partial-alphabetic readers and, 52–53
pre-alphabetic readers and, 51–52